Magical Christmas

Adult Coloring Book

CREATIVE COLORING PRESS

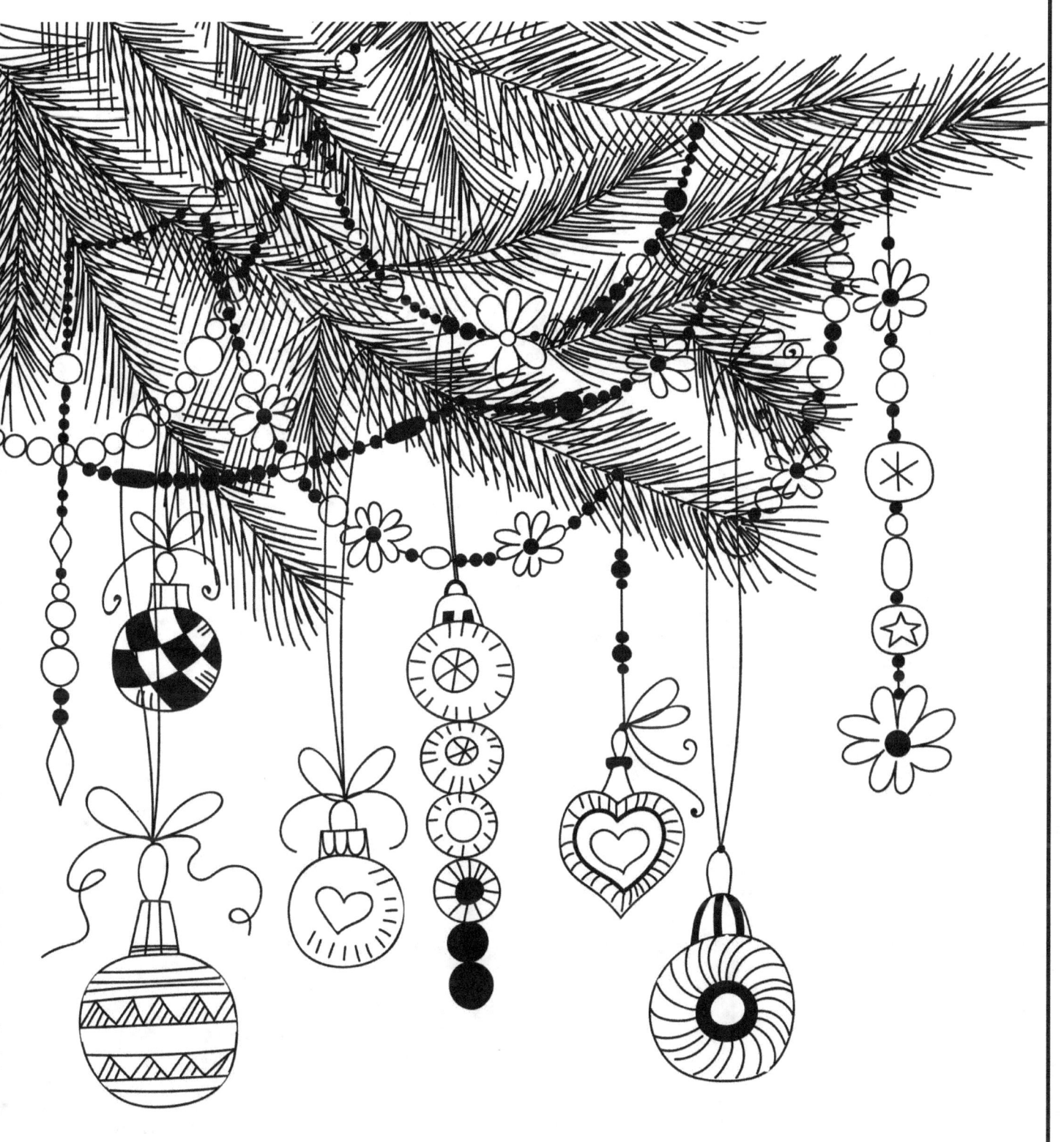

Merry Christmas

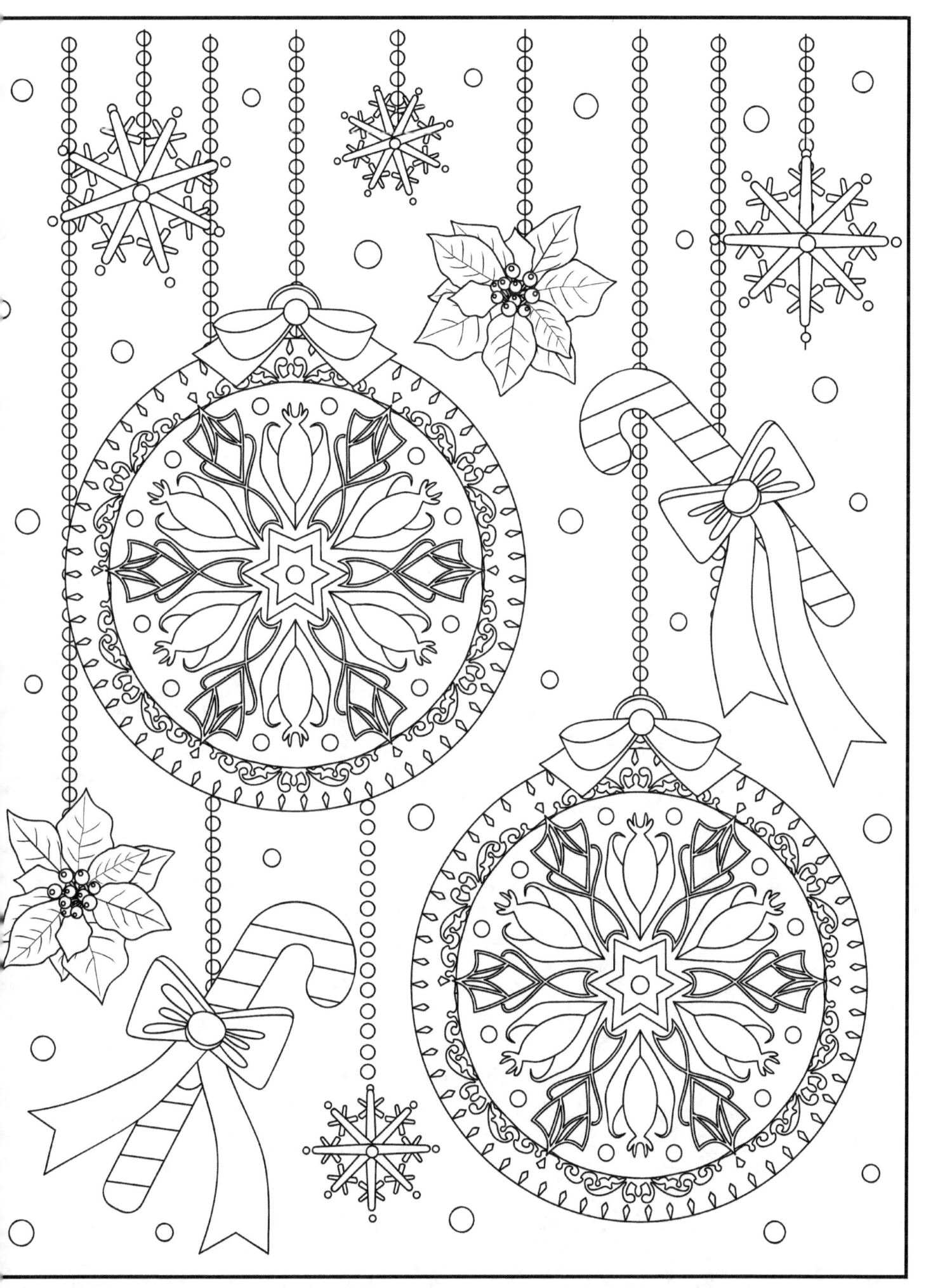

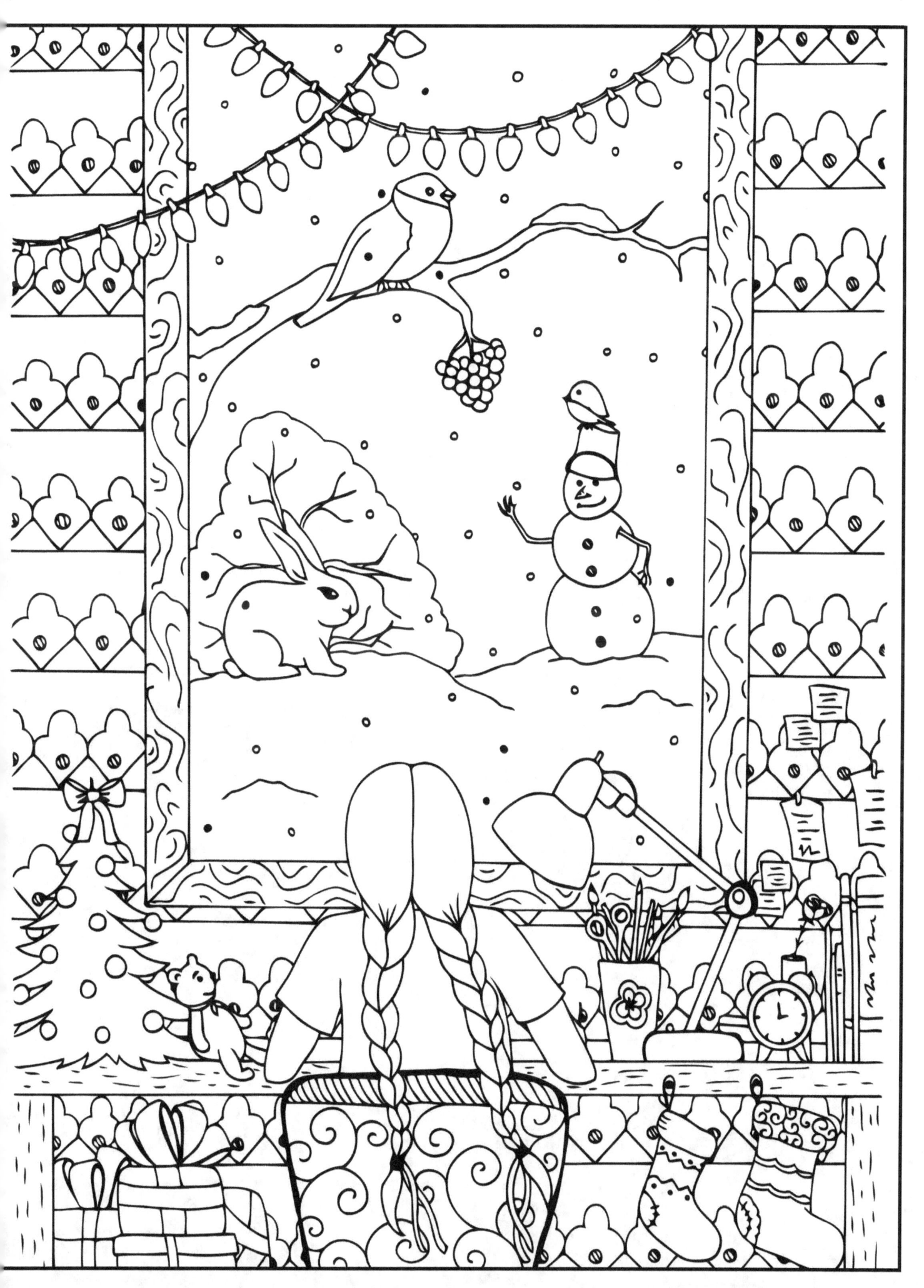

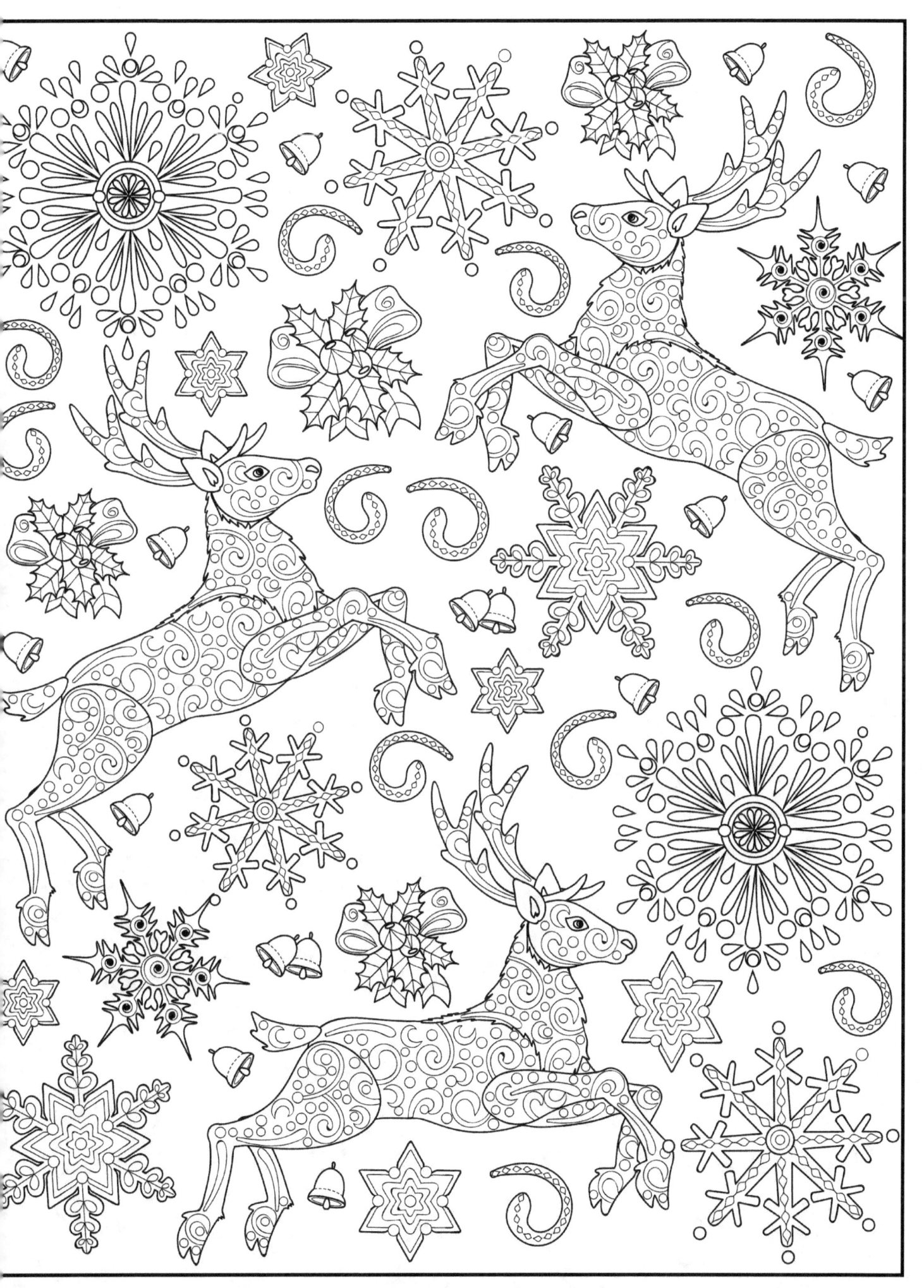

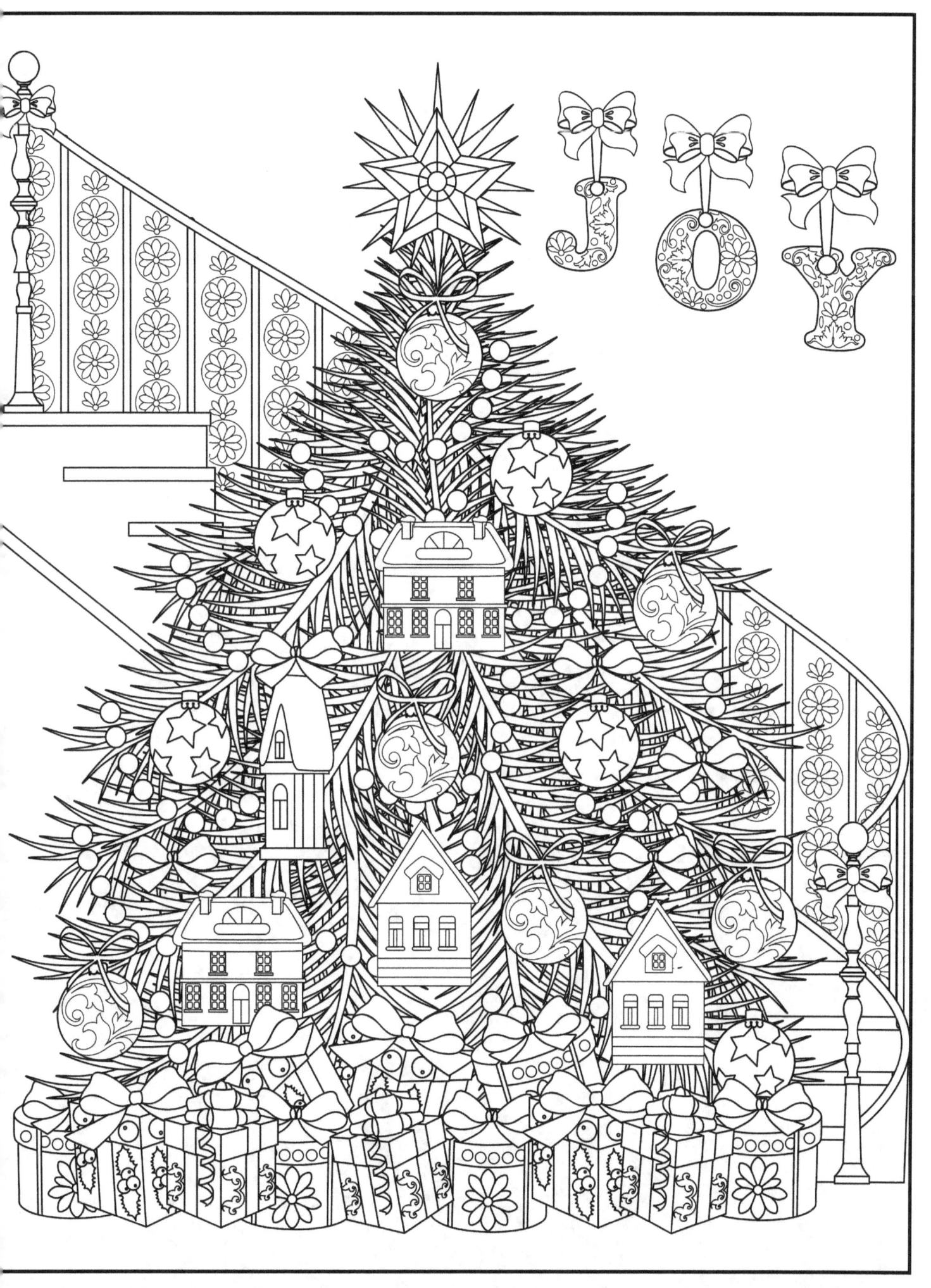

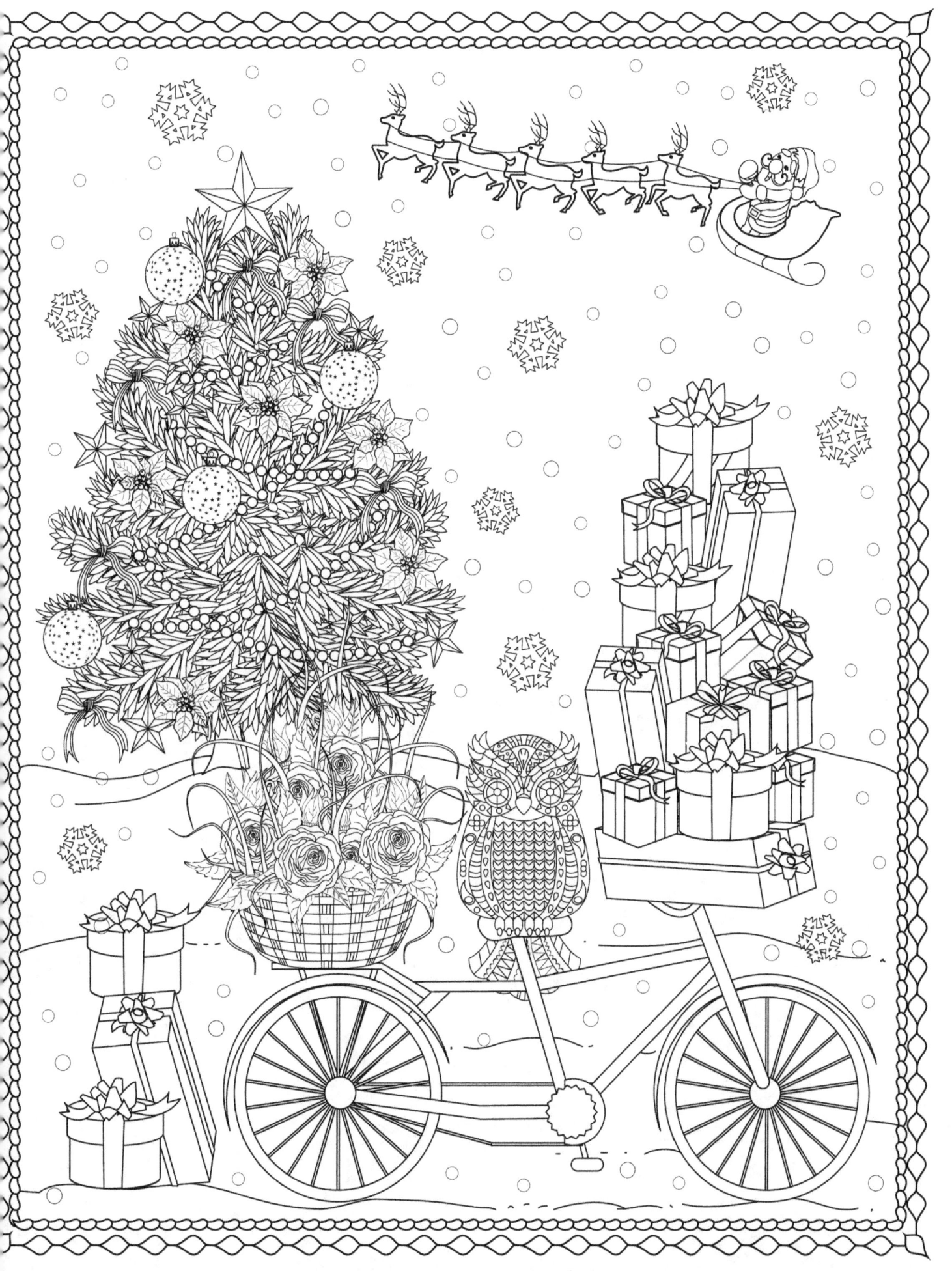

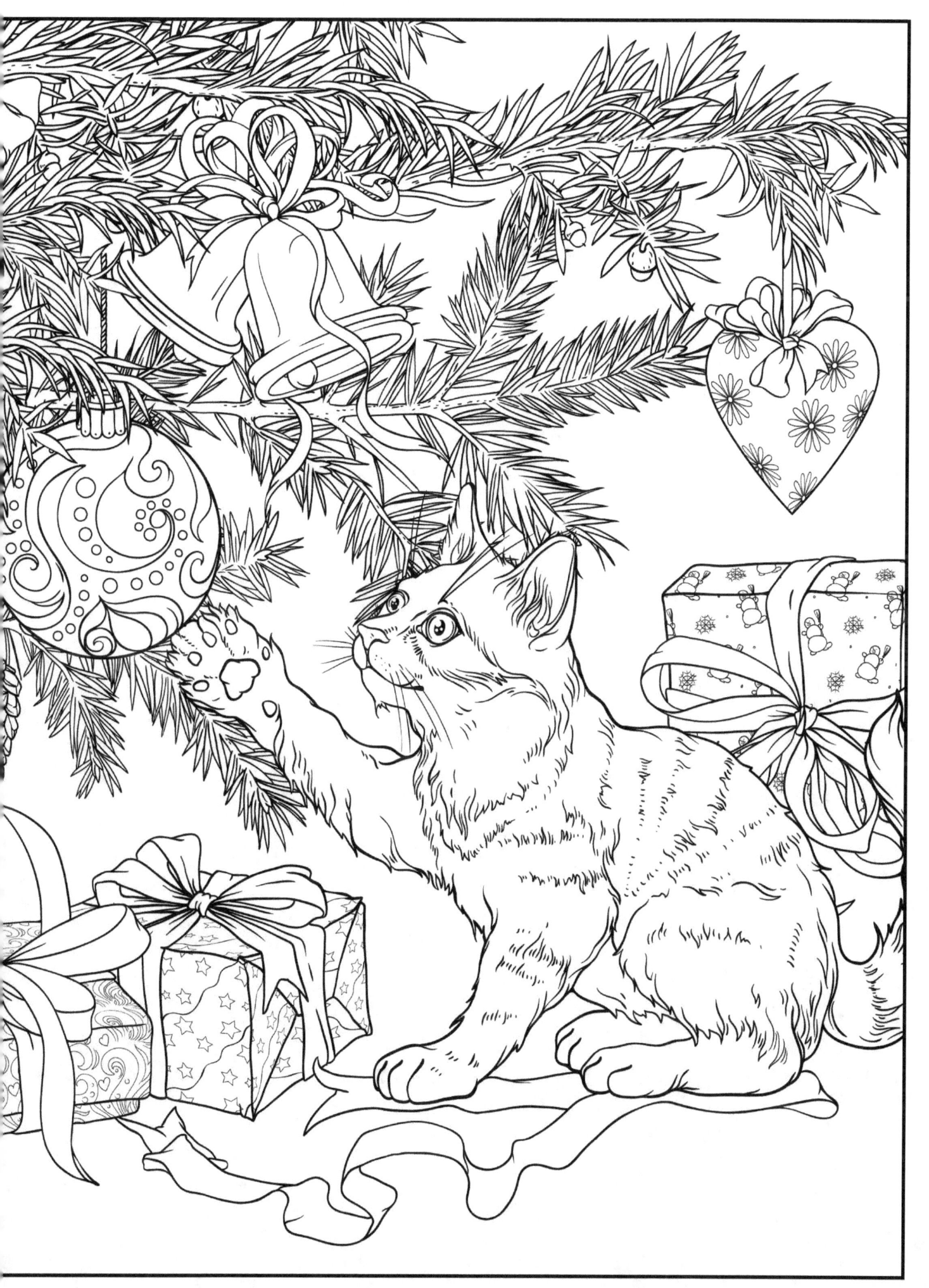

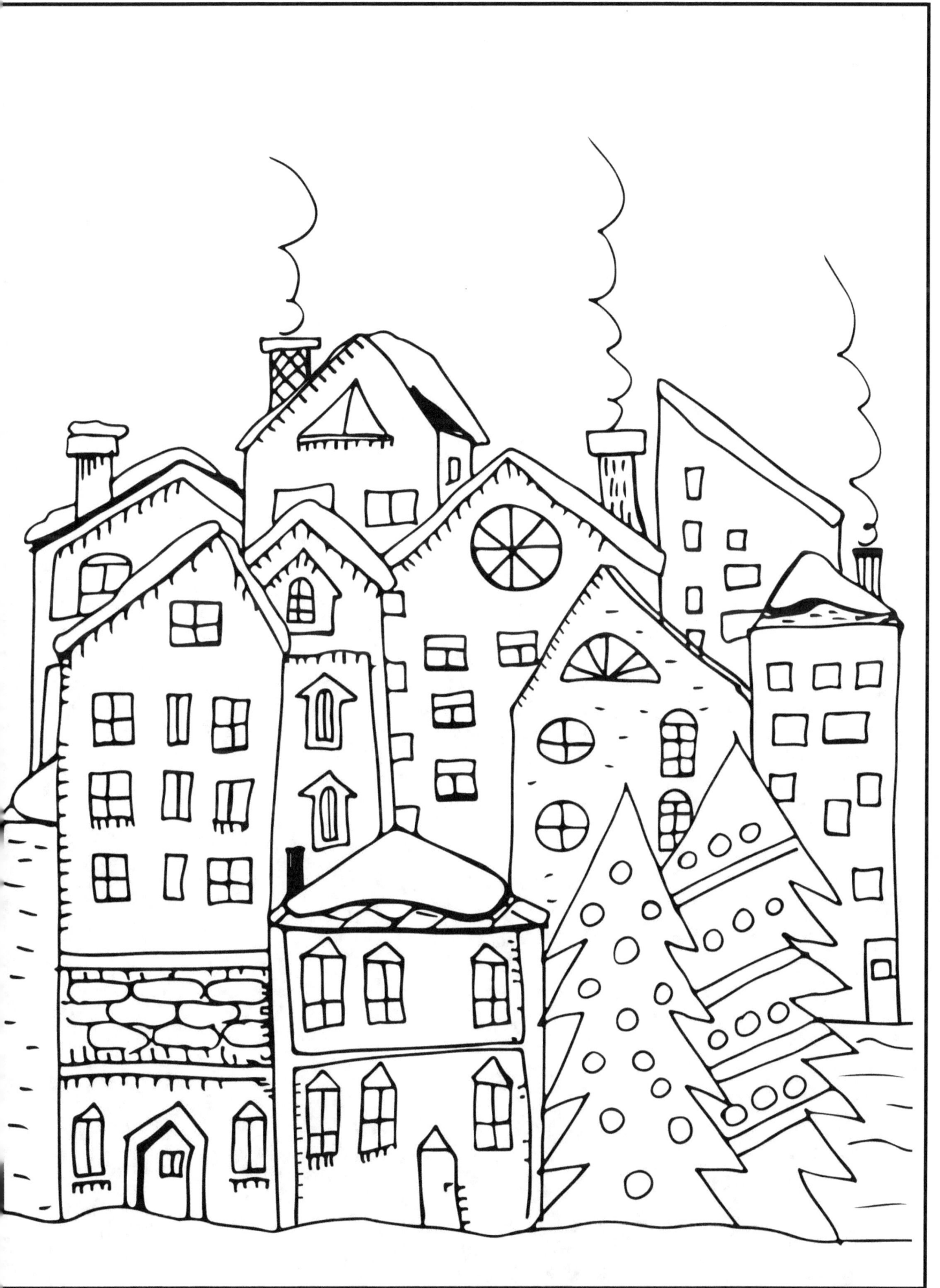

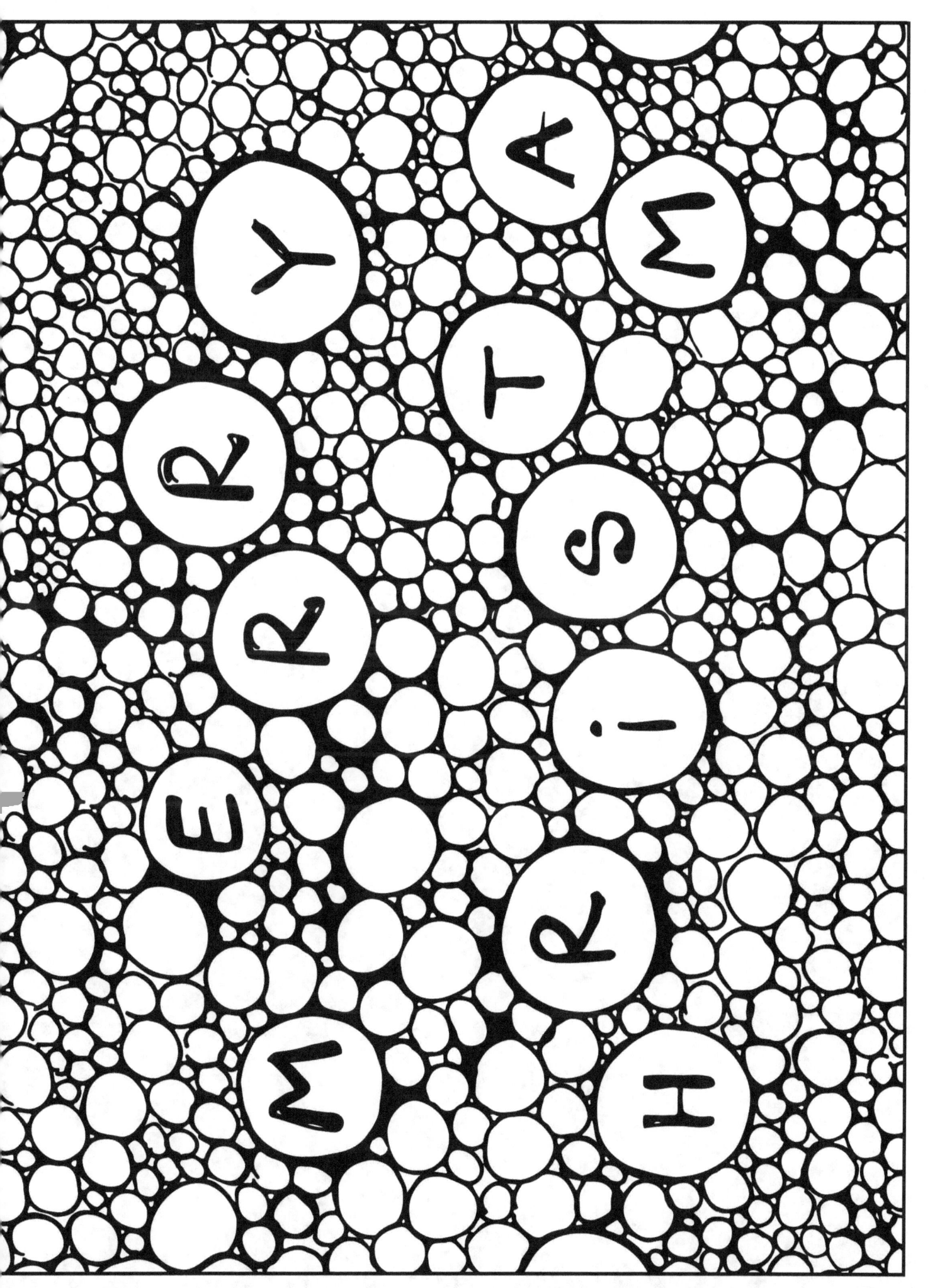

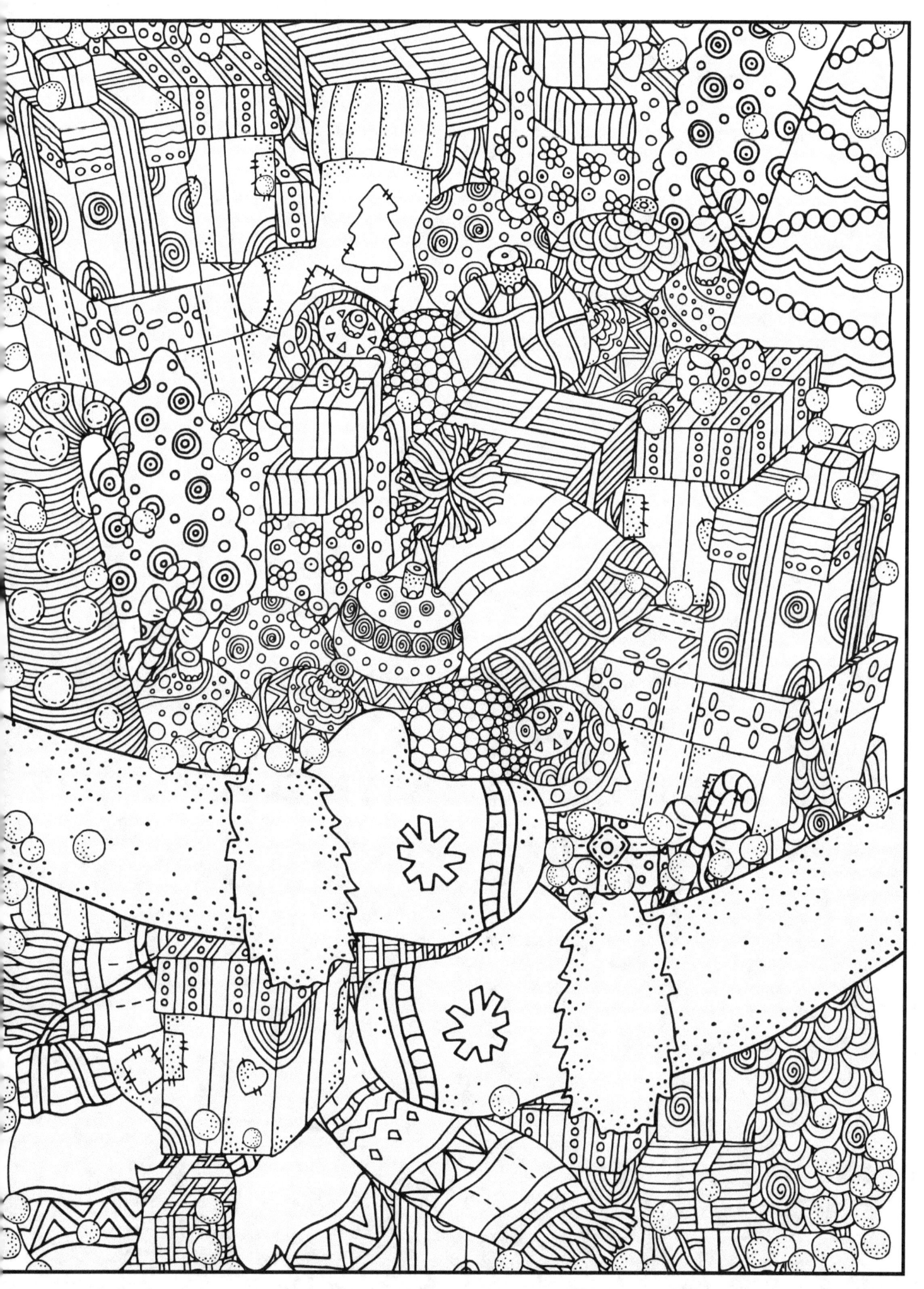

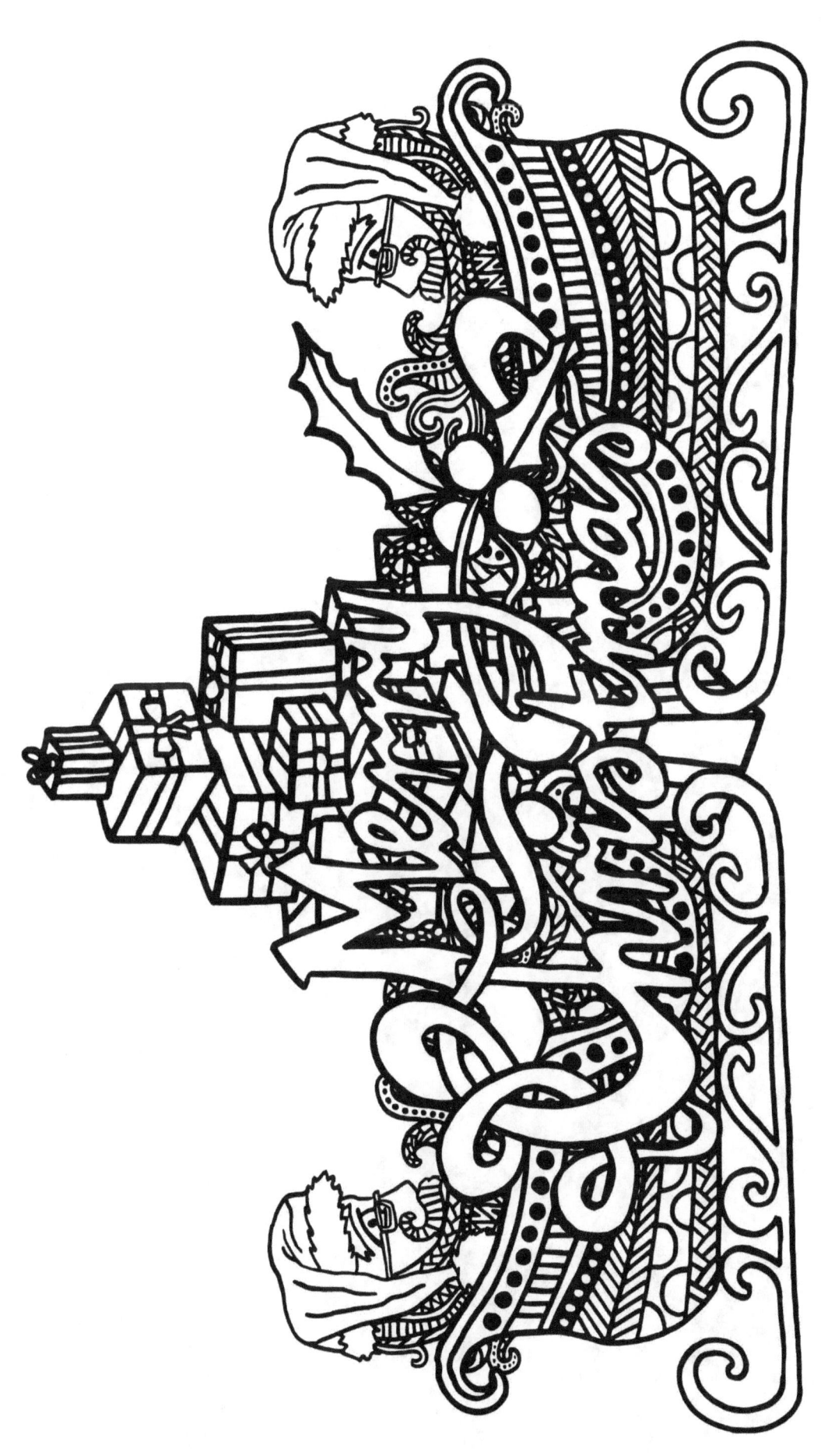

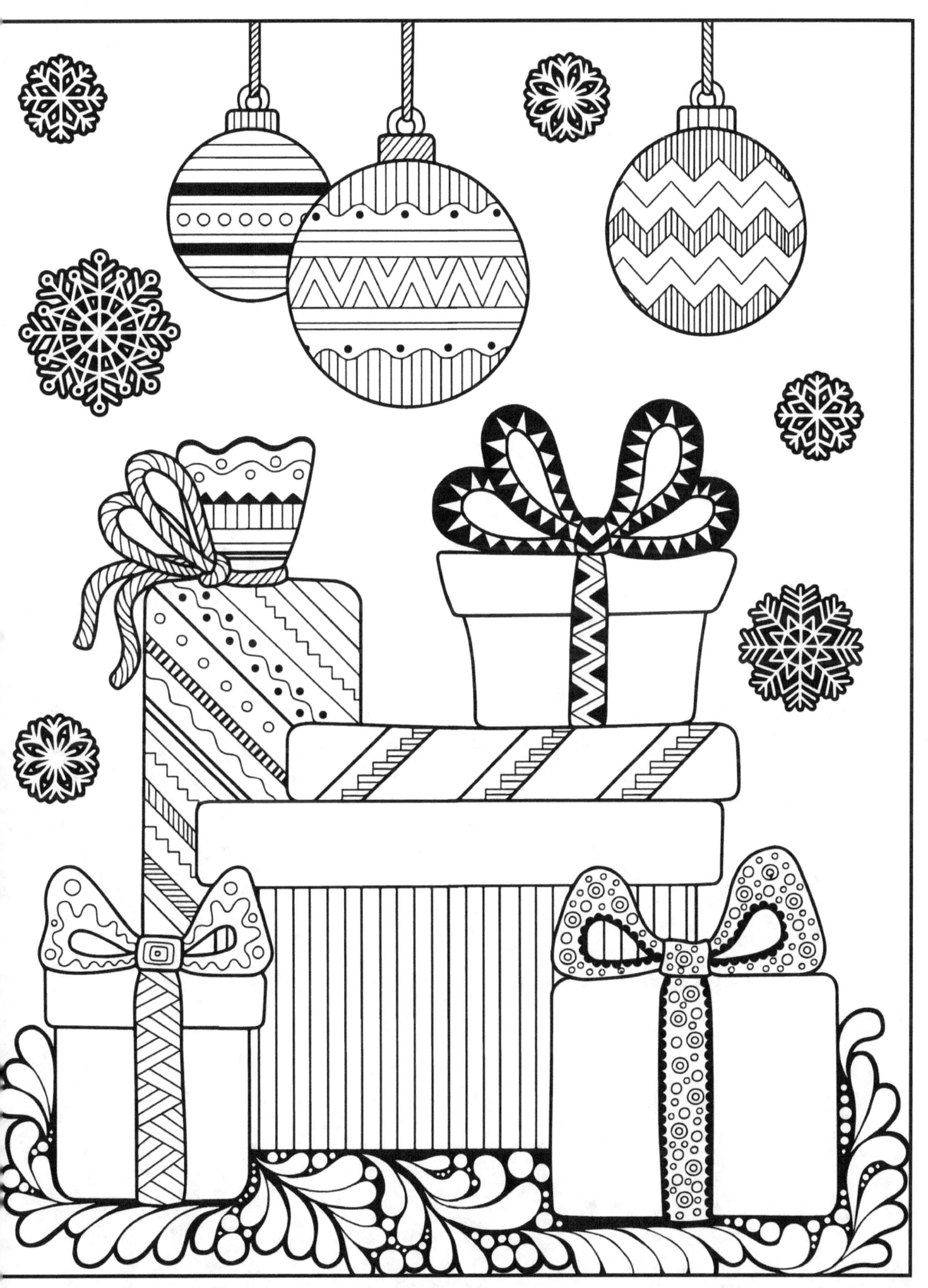

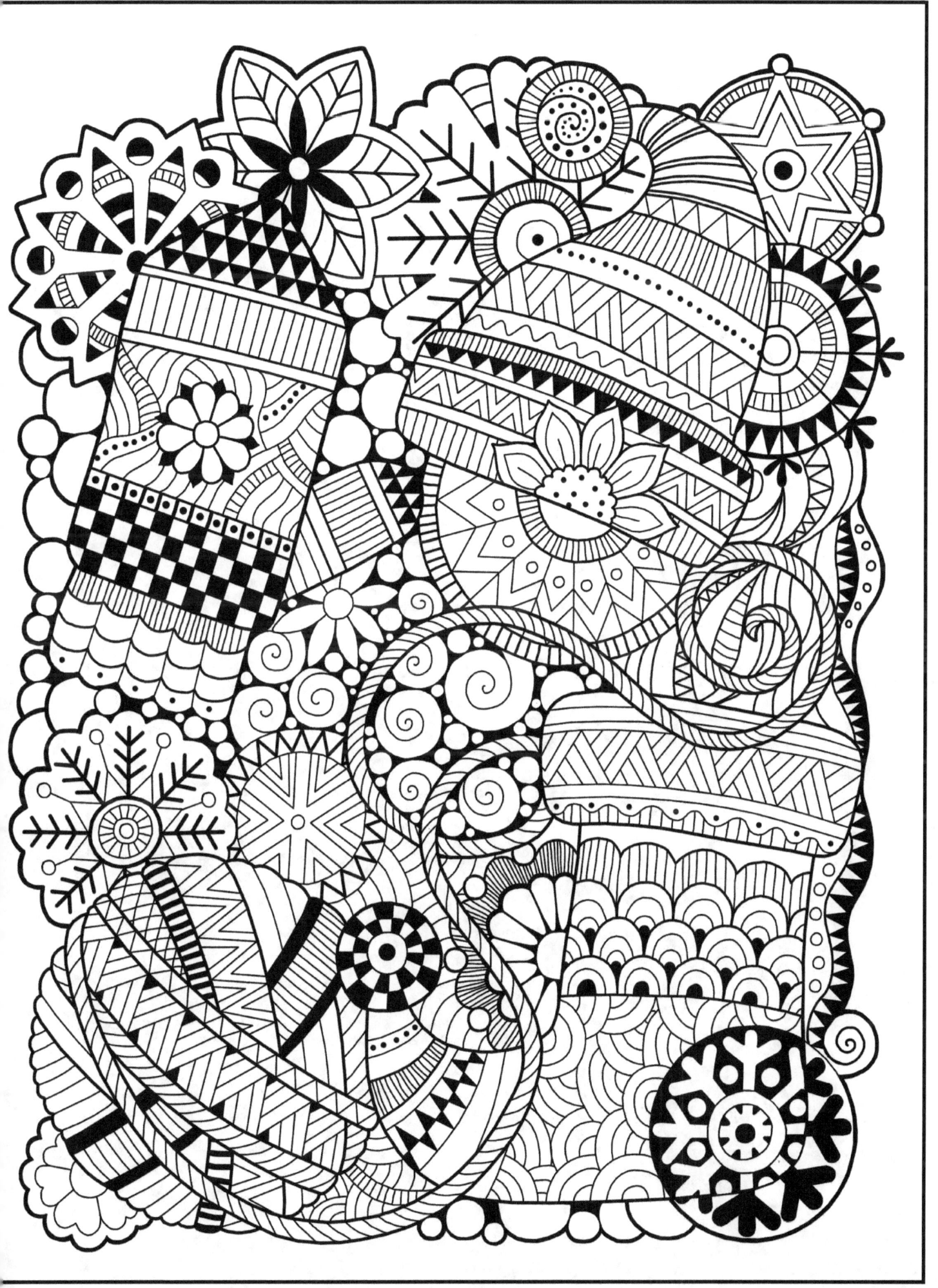

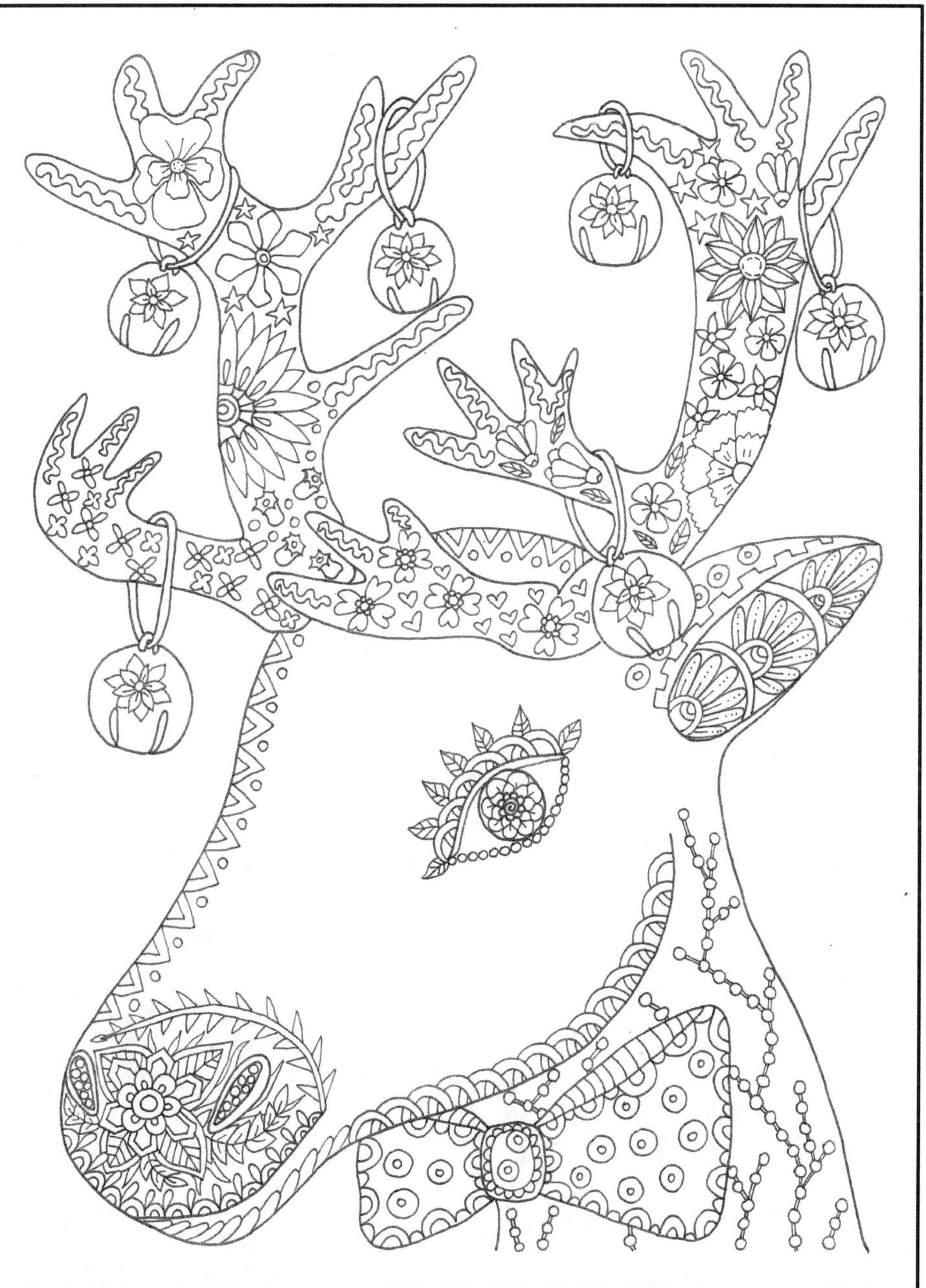

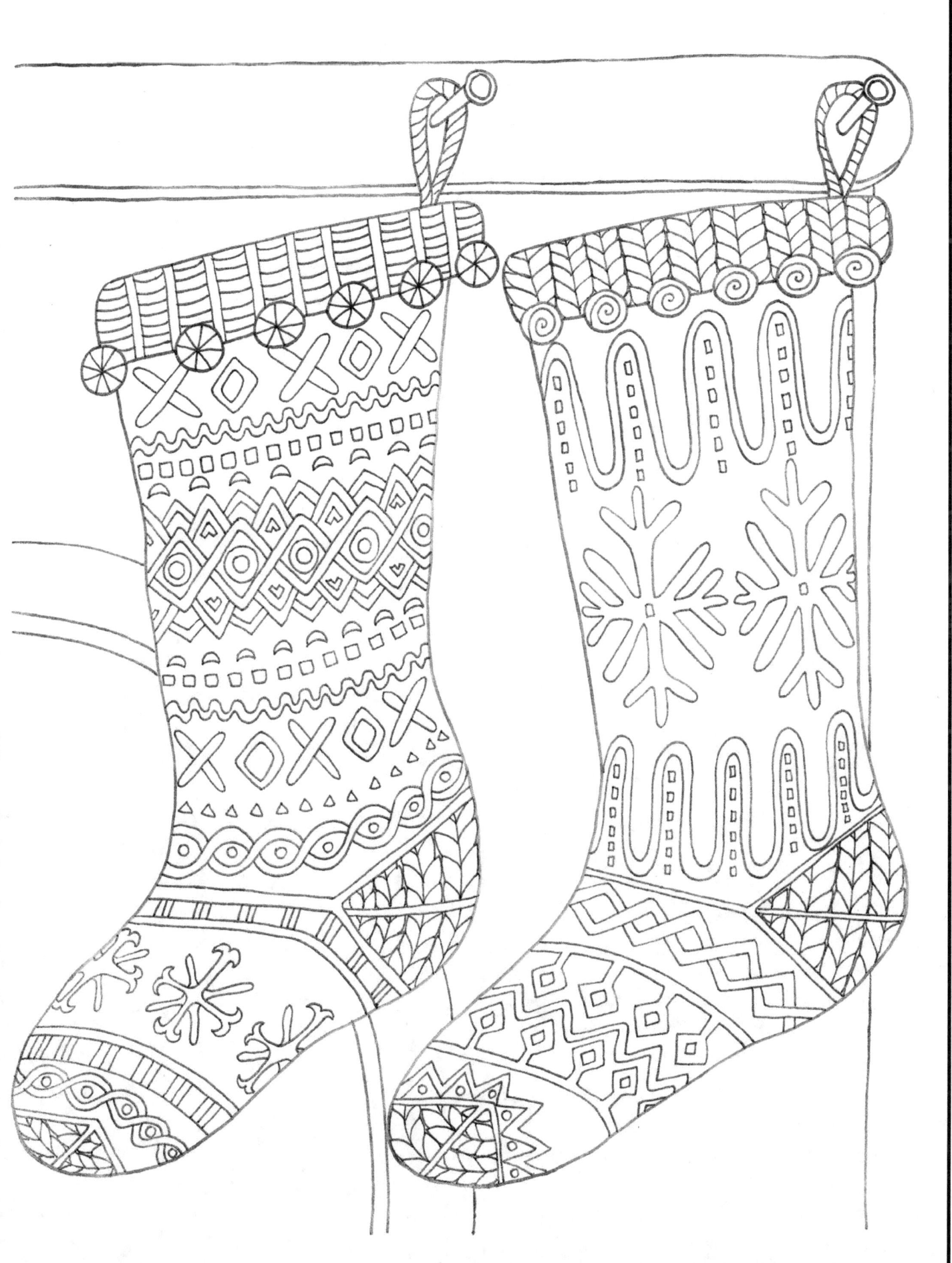

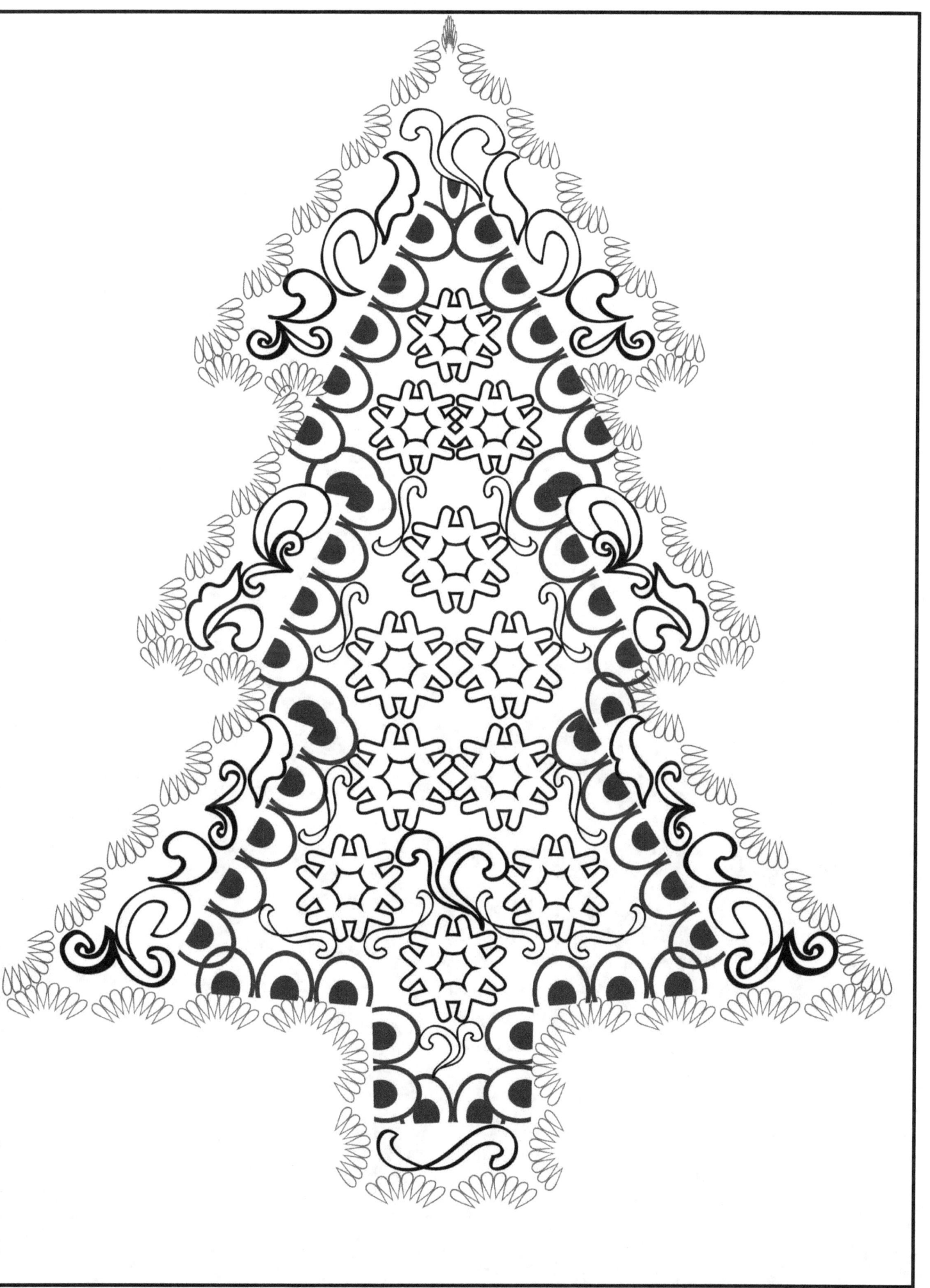

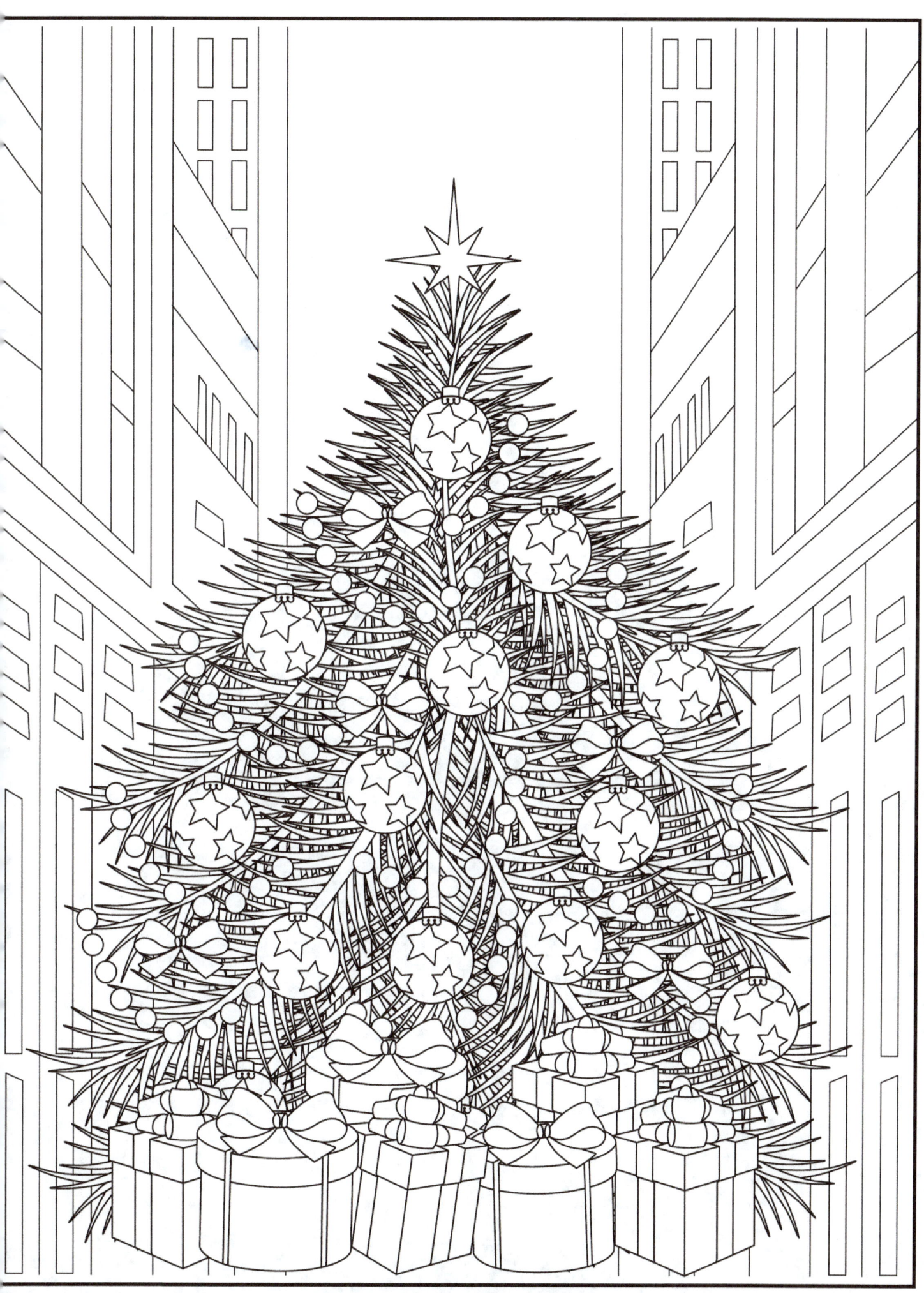

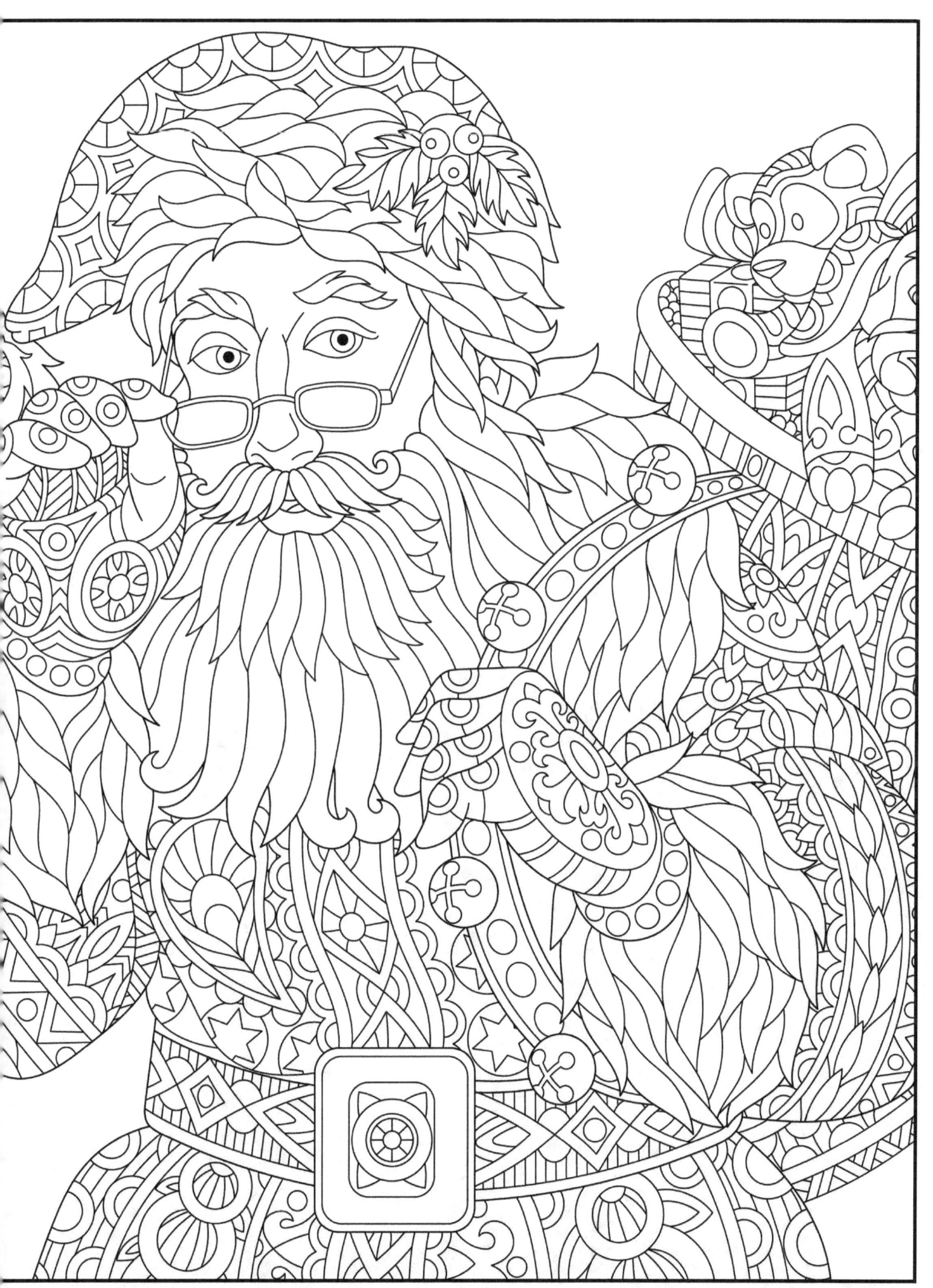

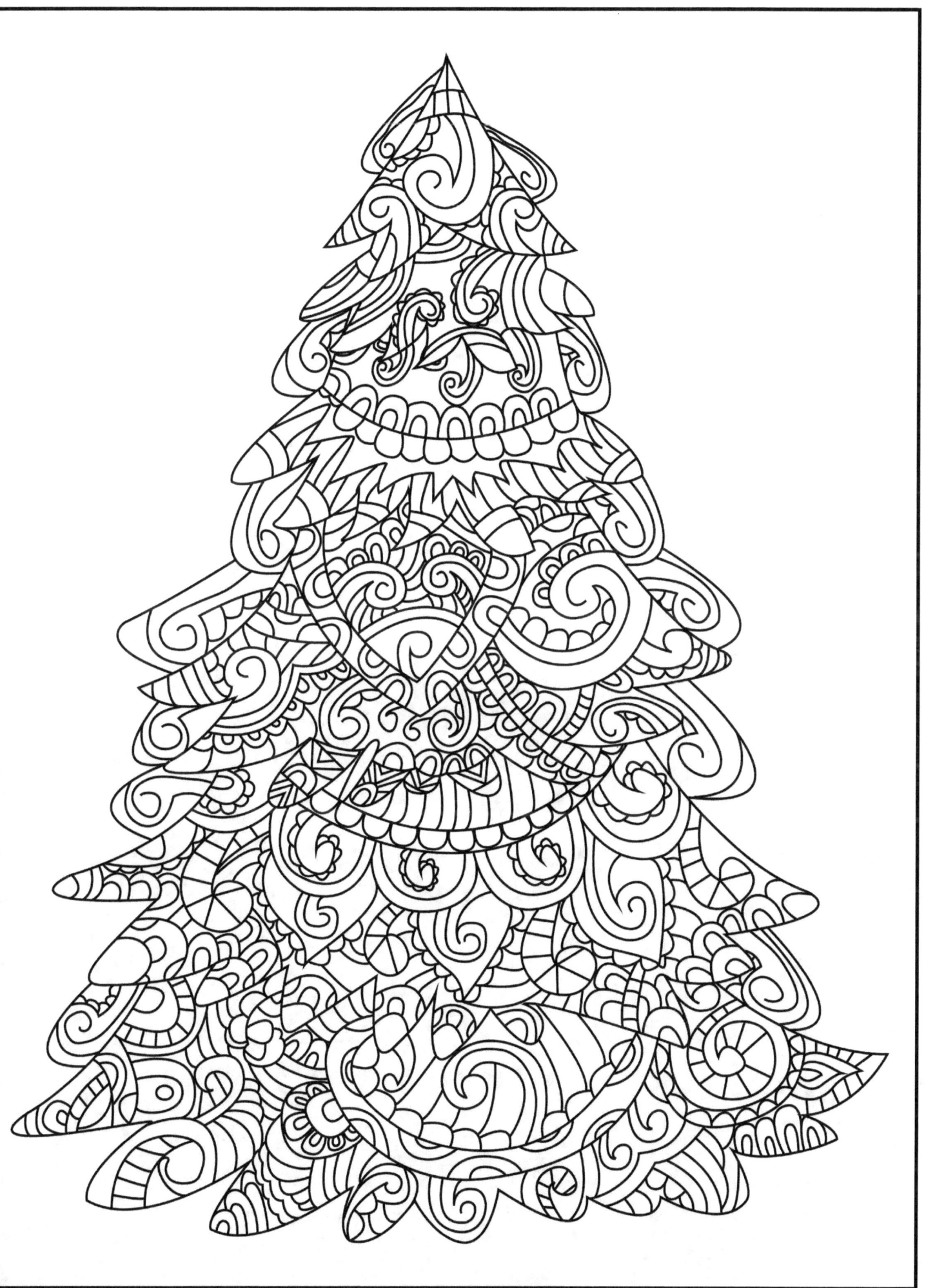

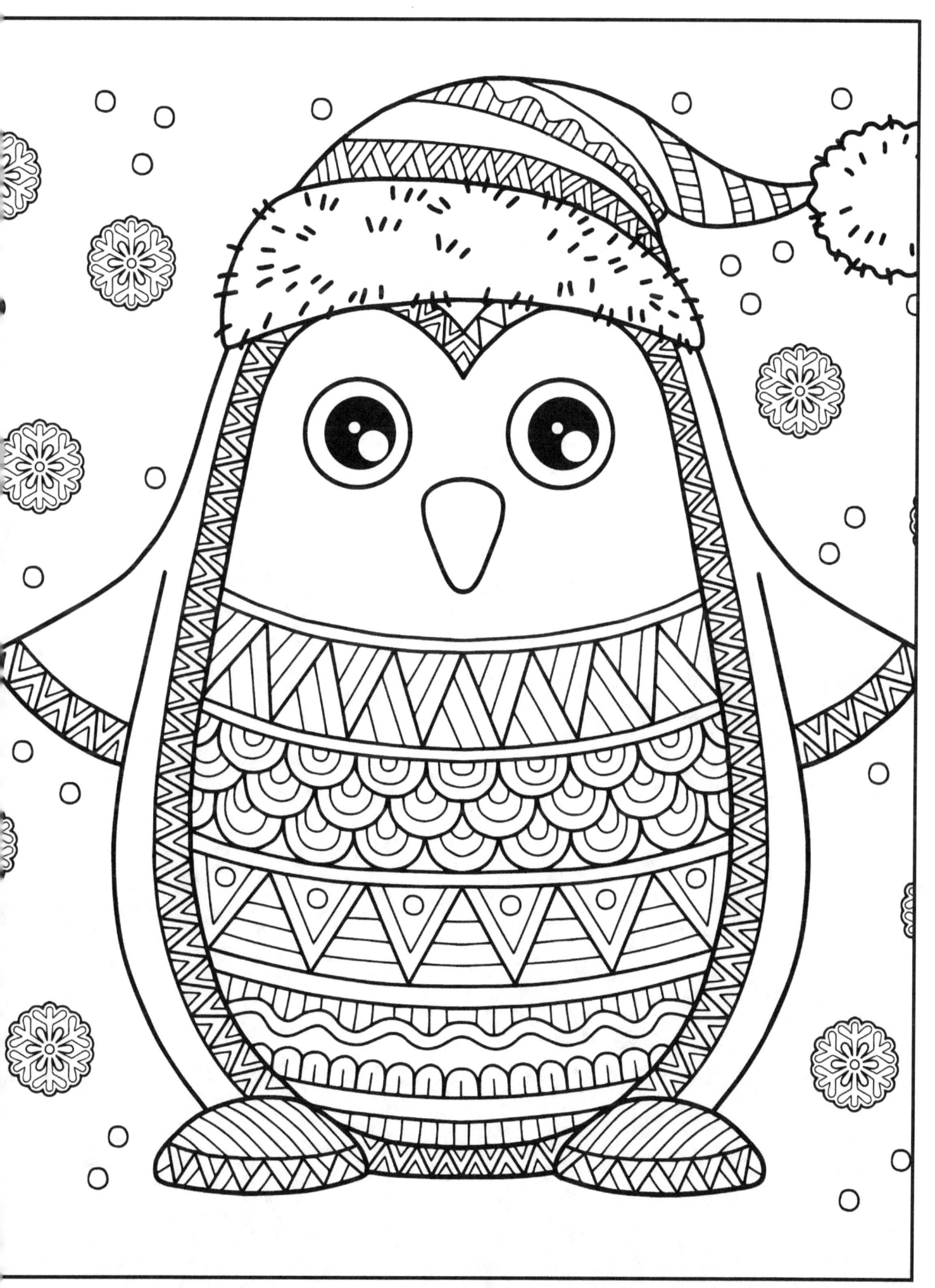

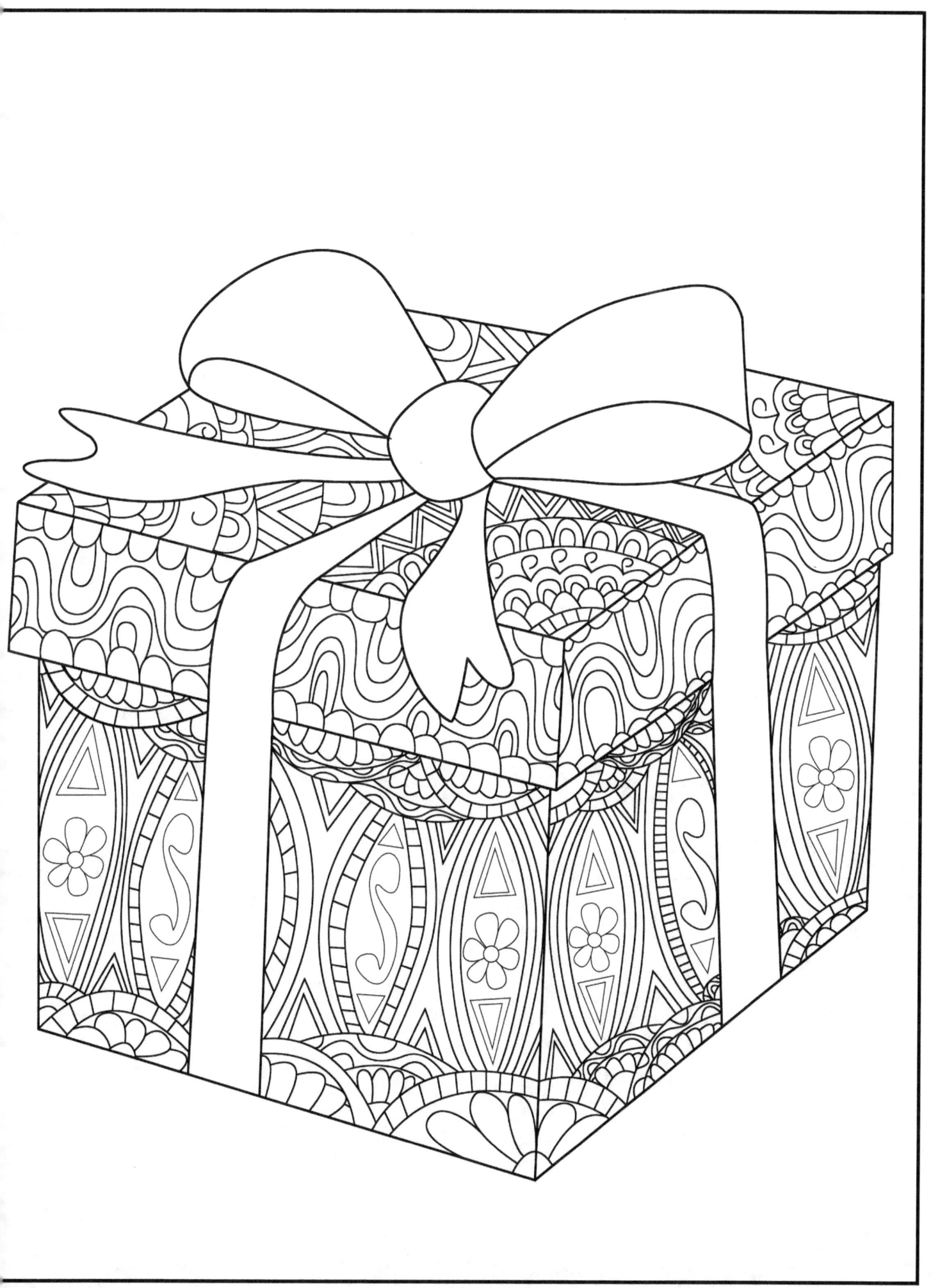

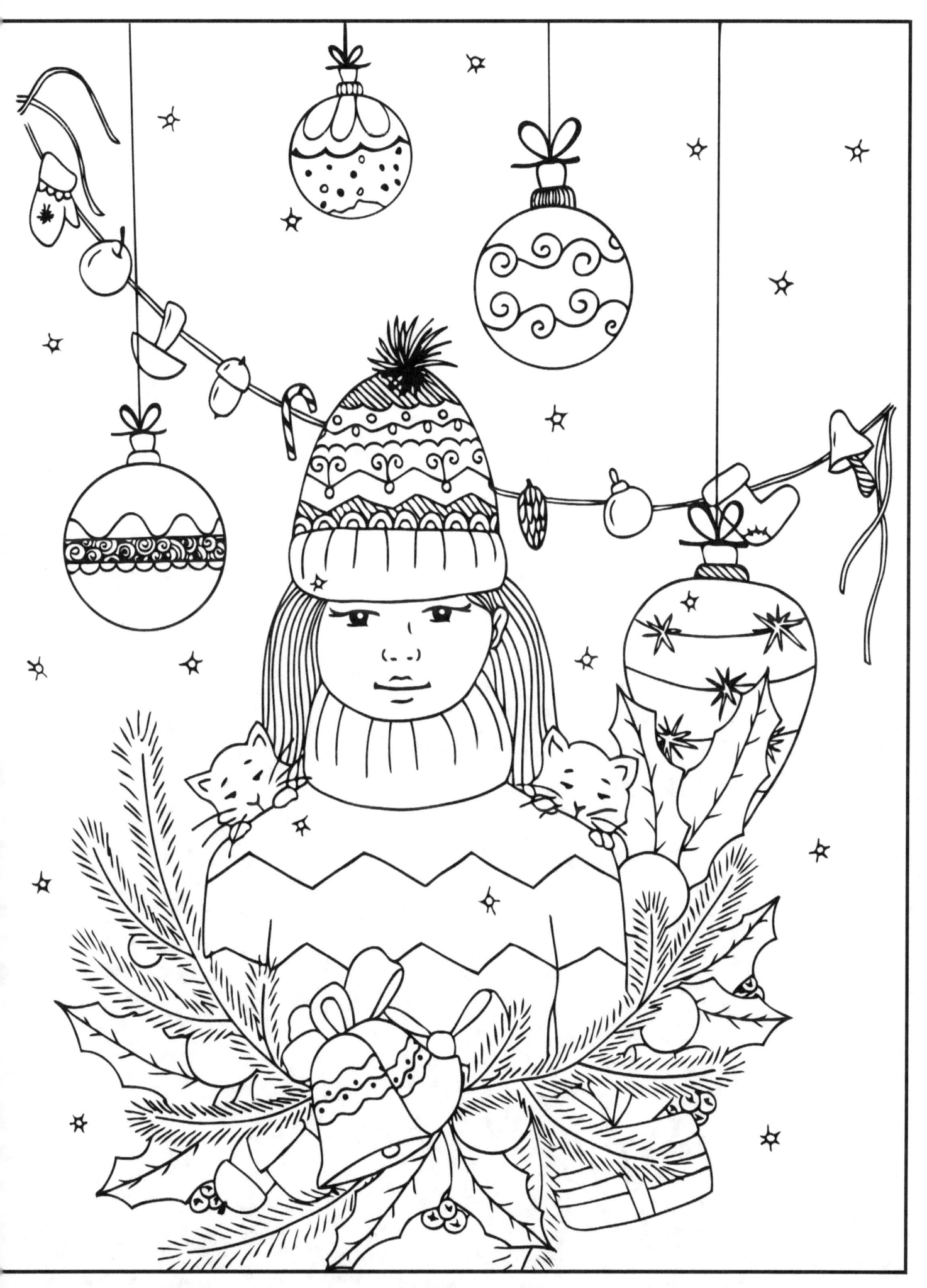

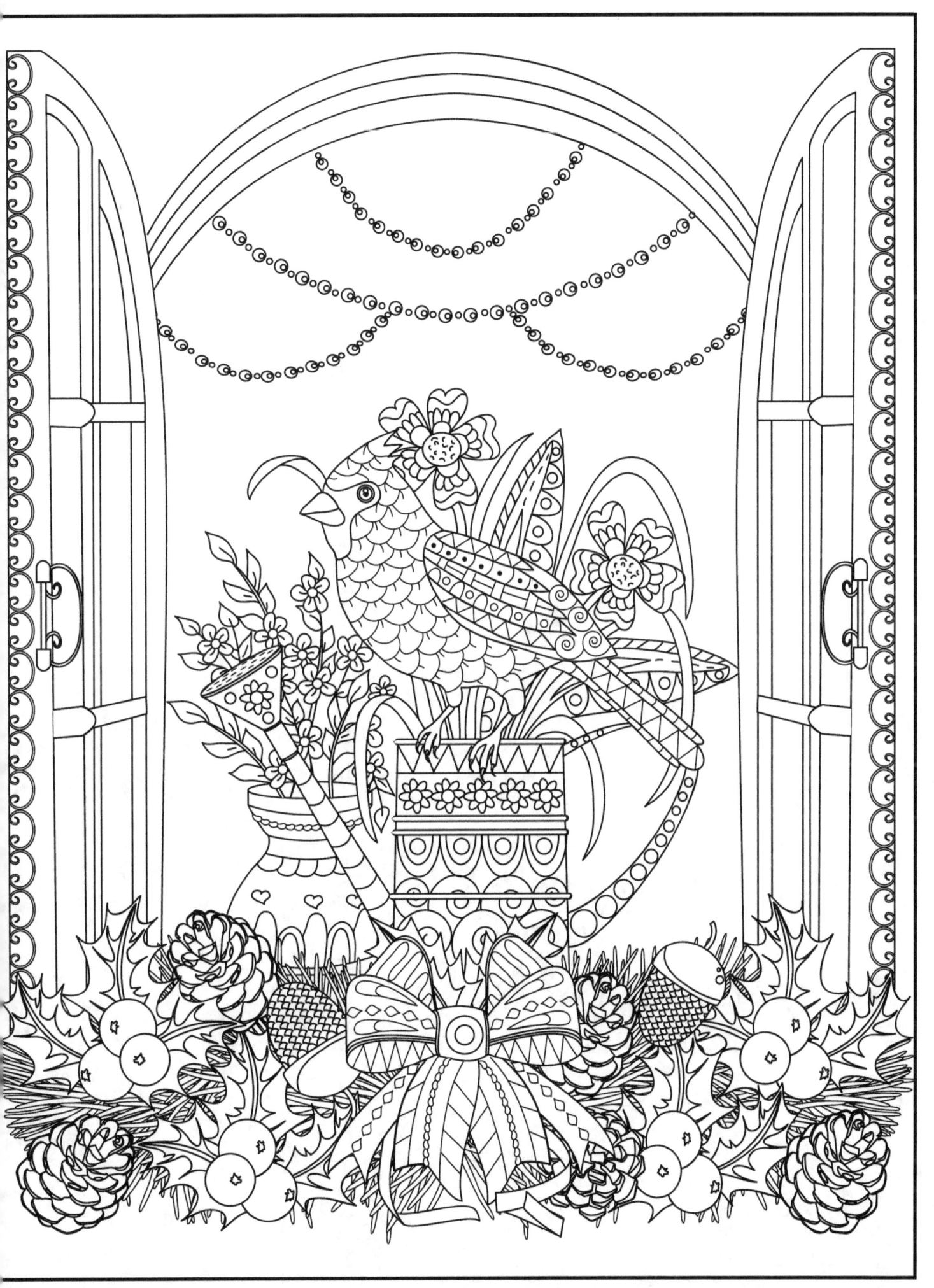

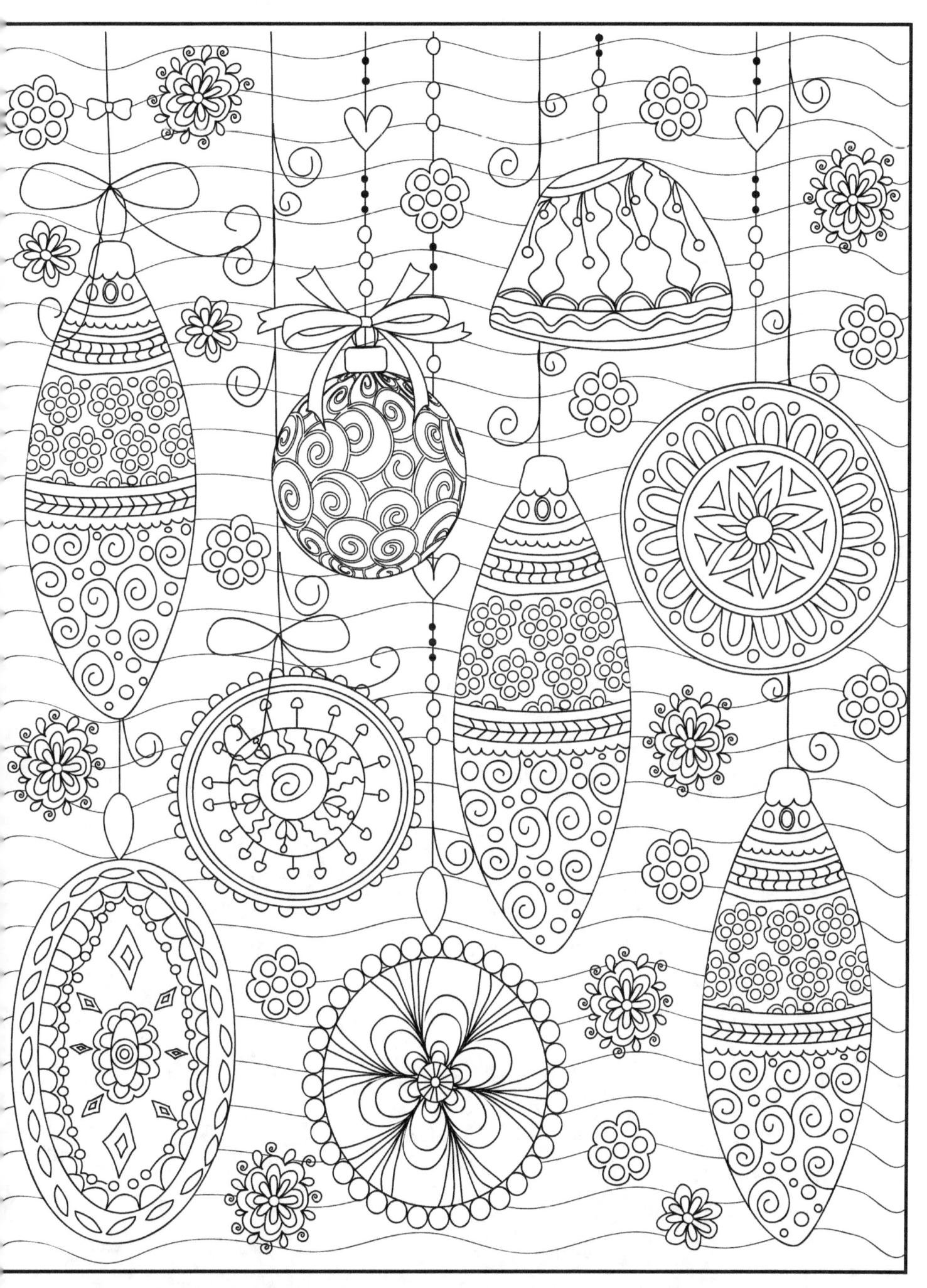

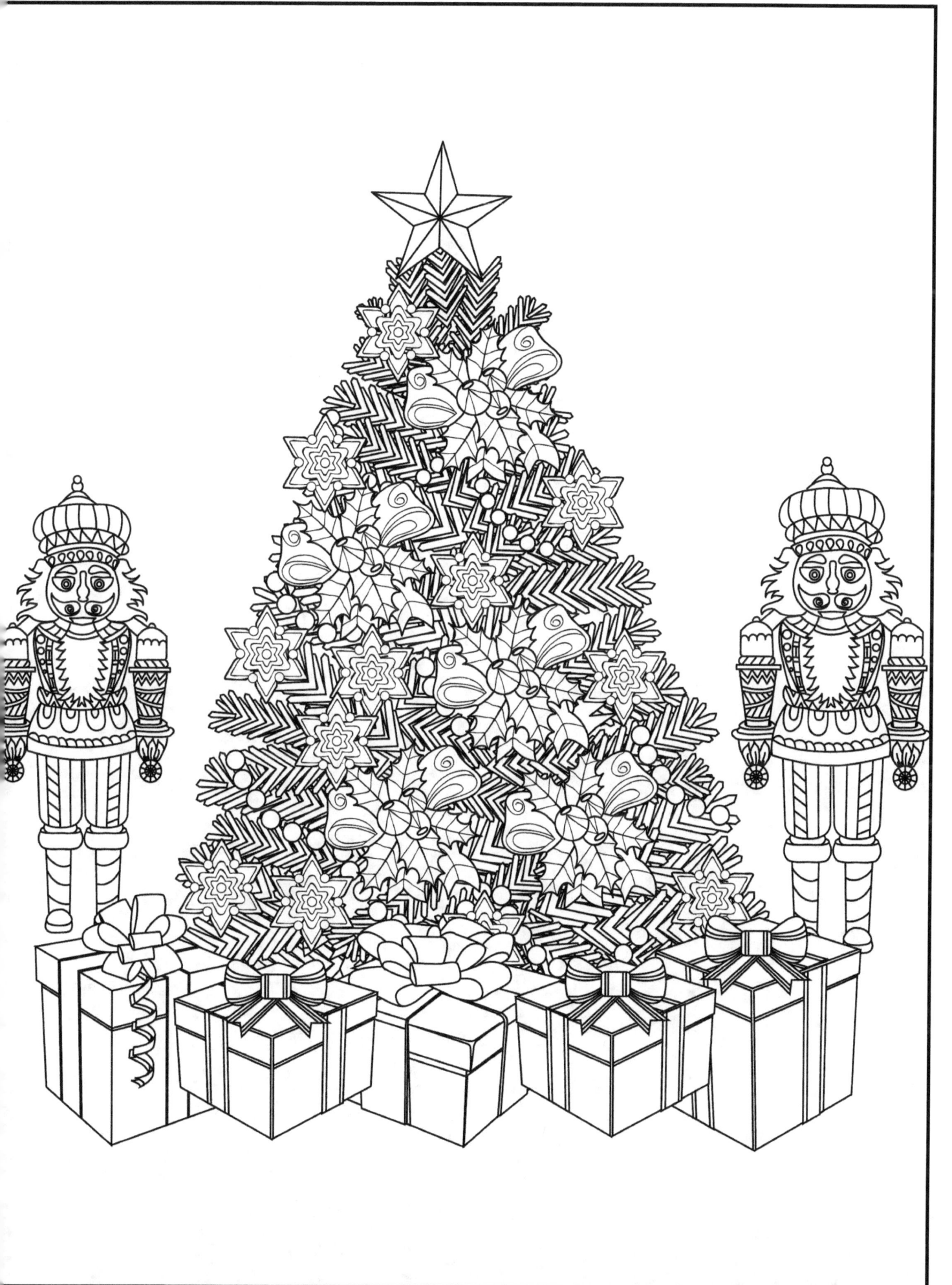

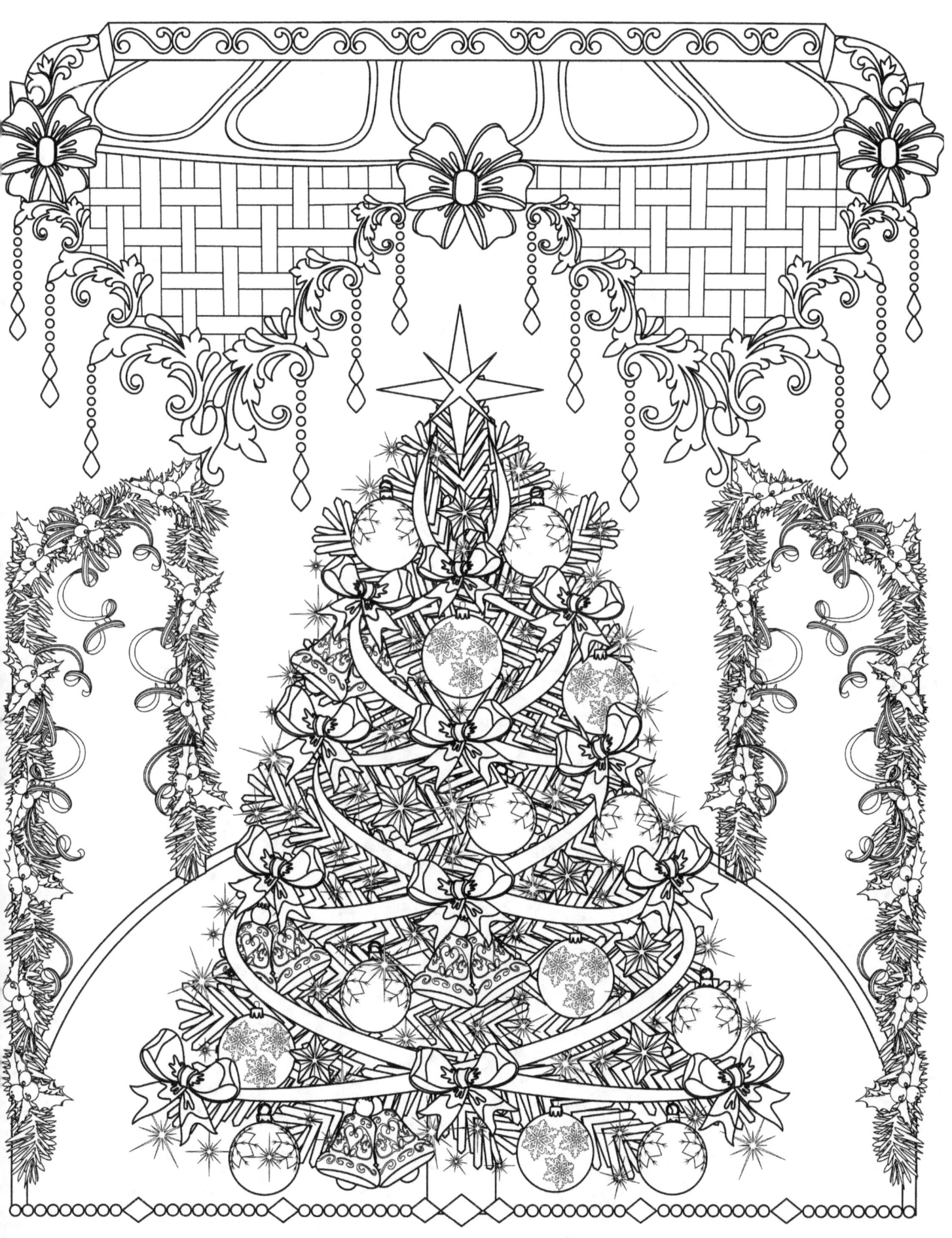

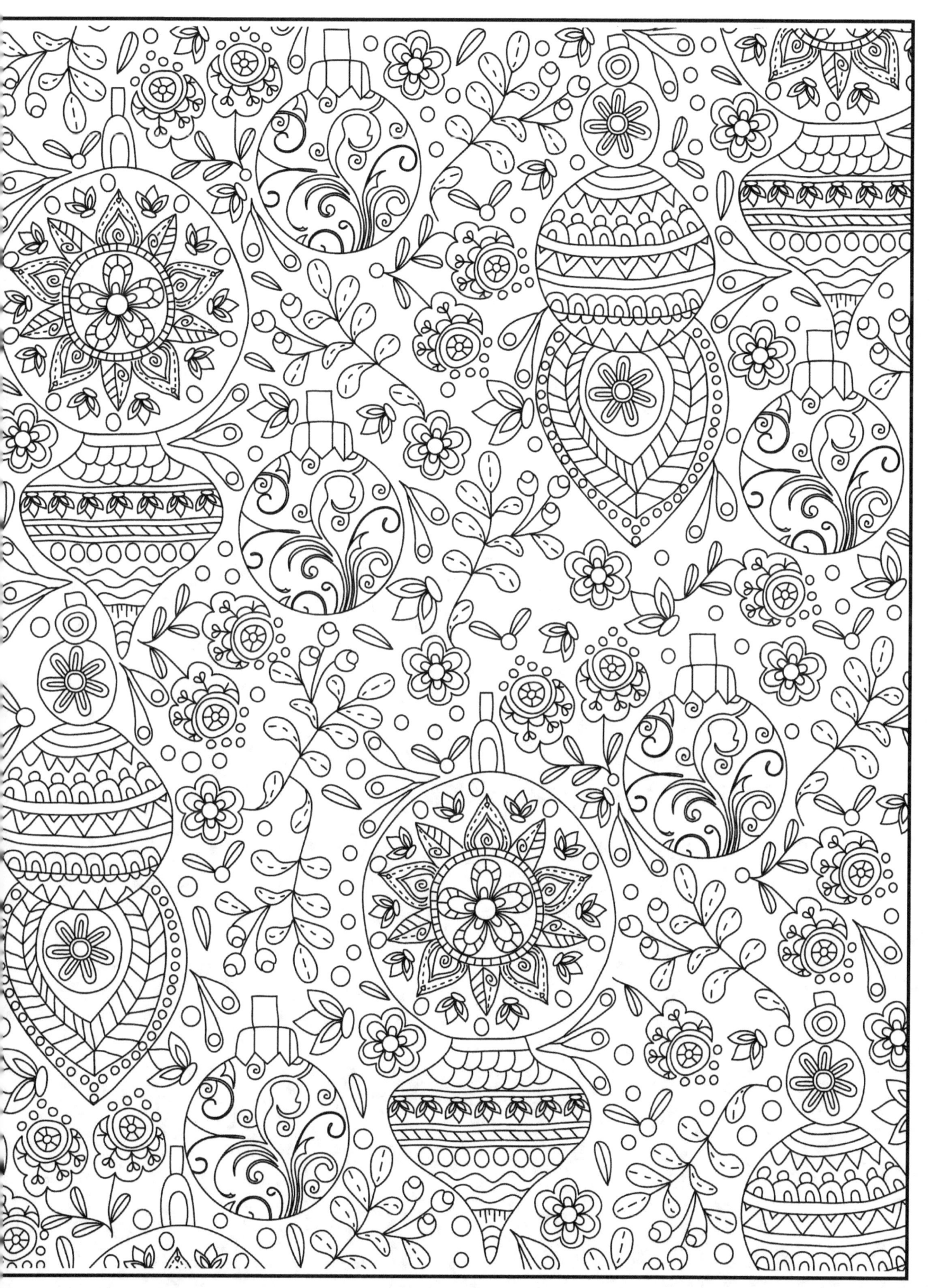

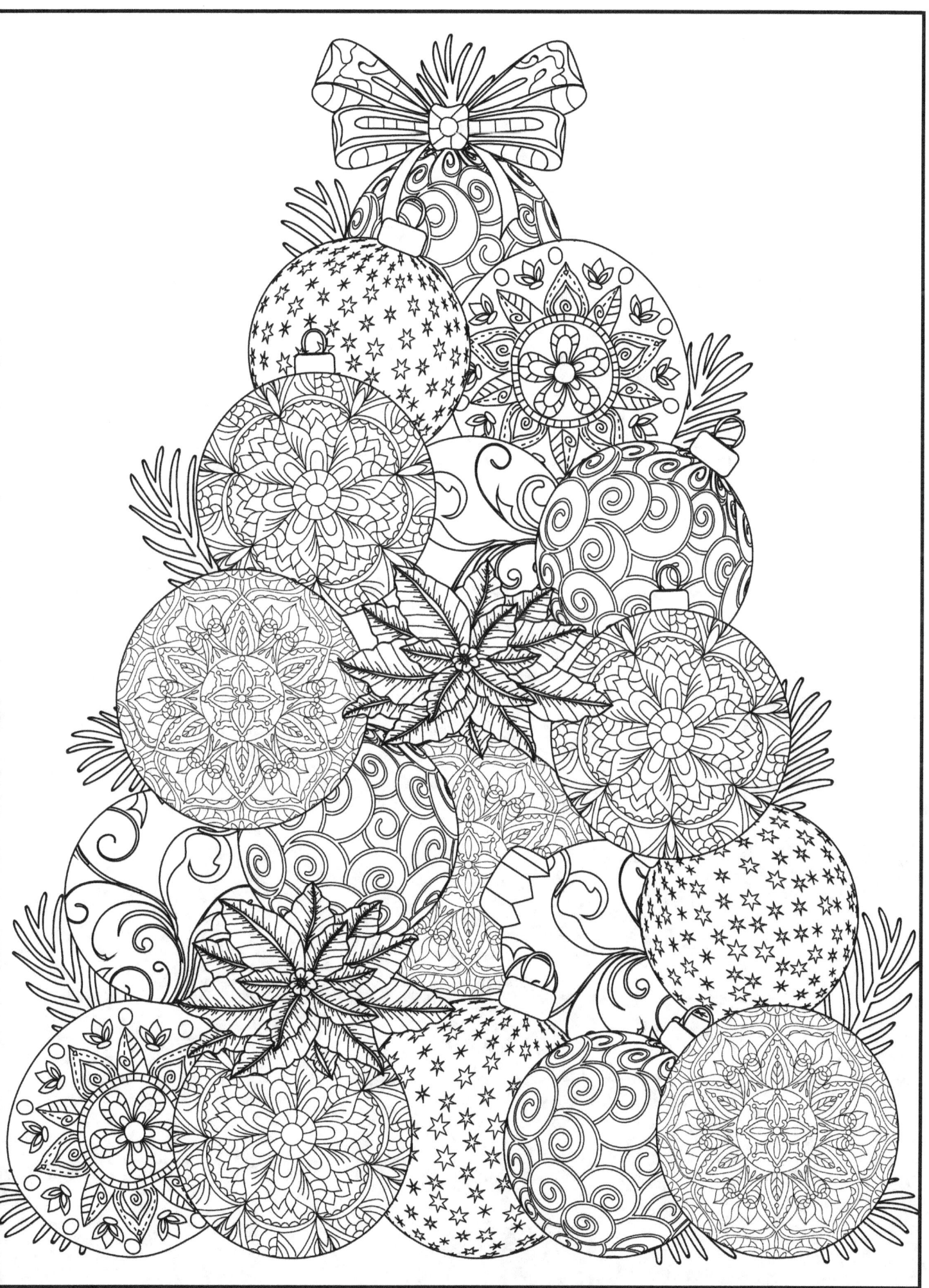

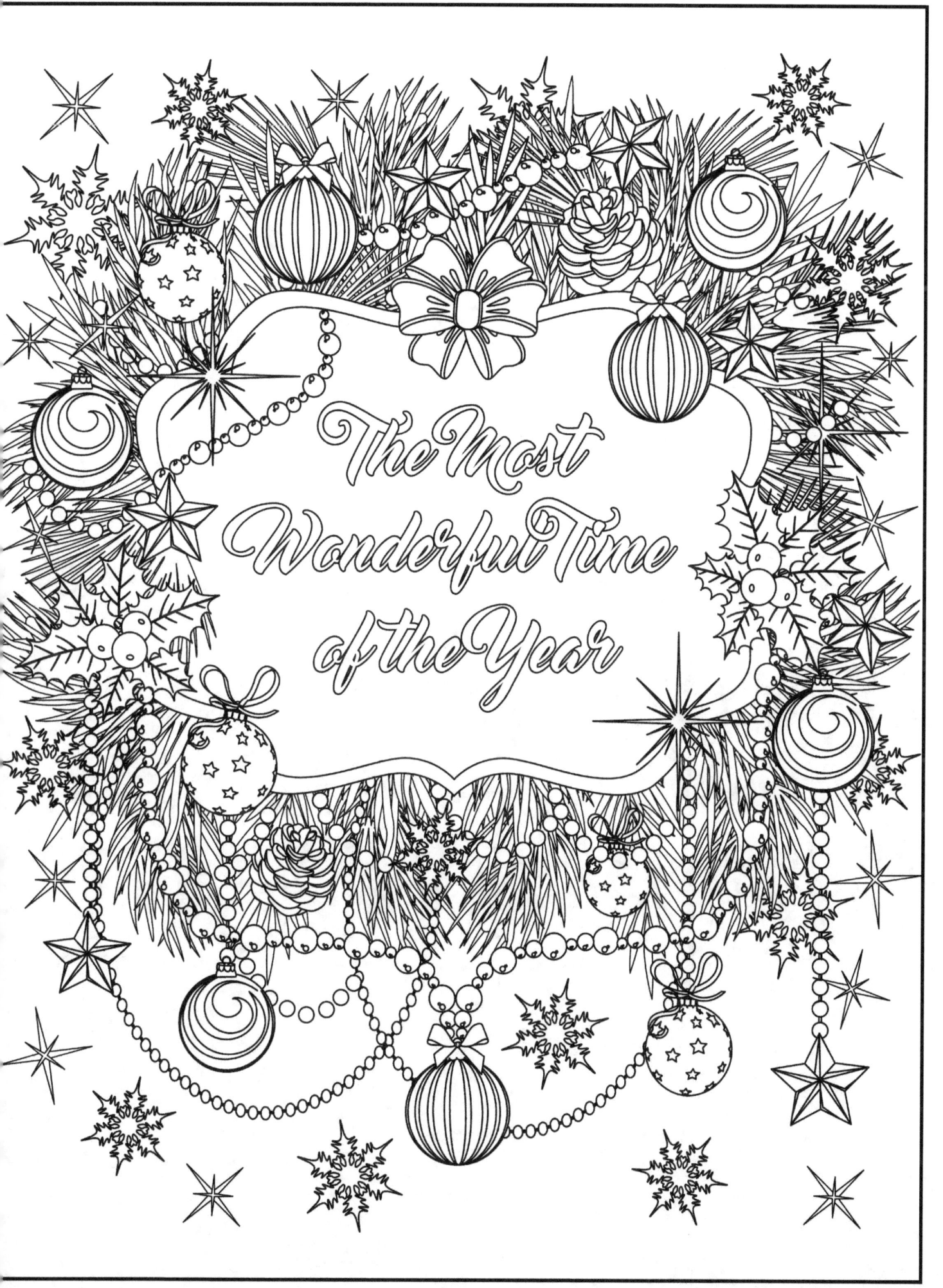

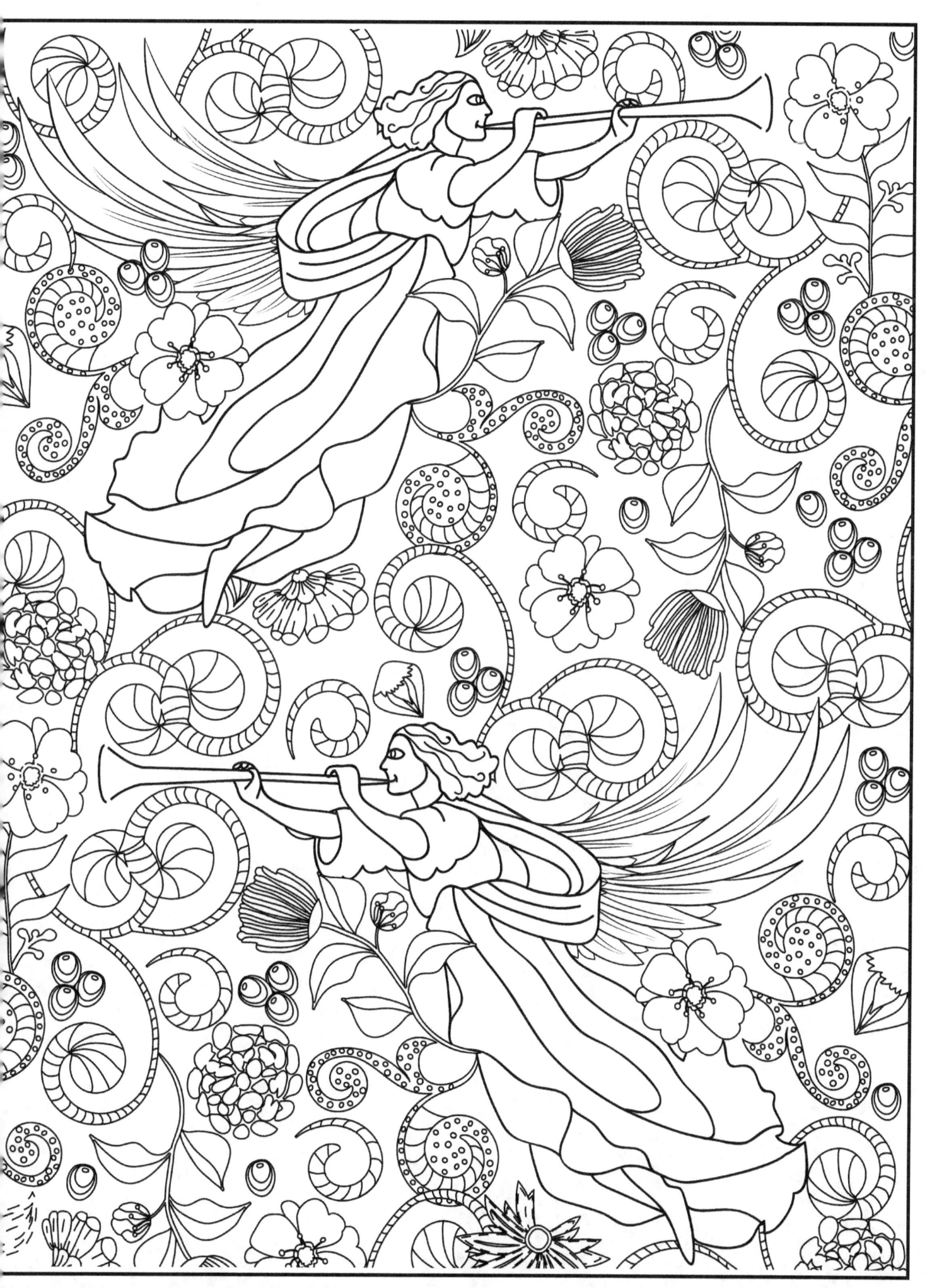

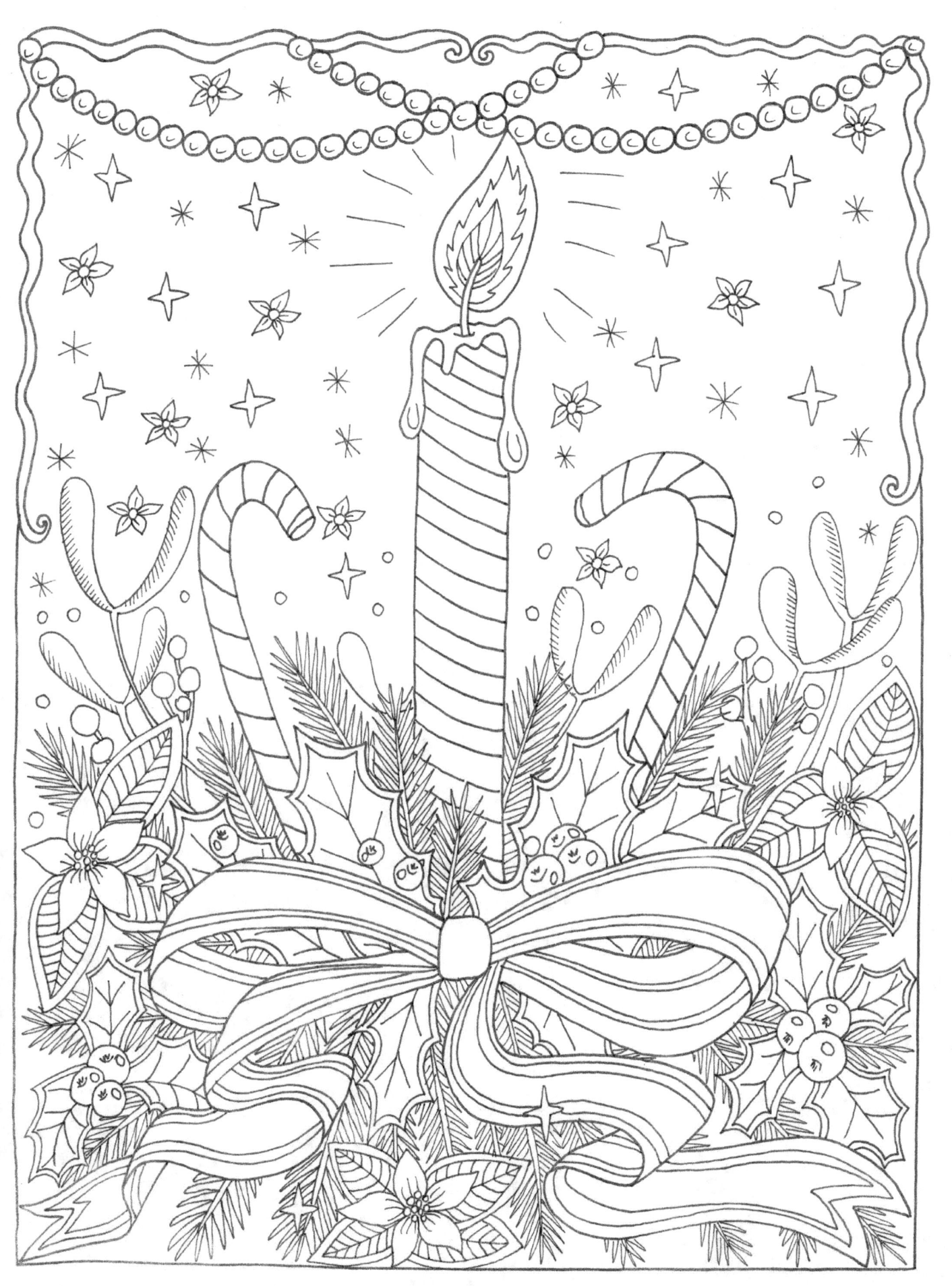

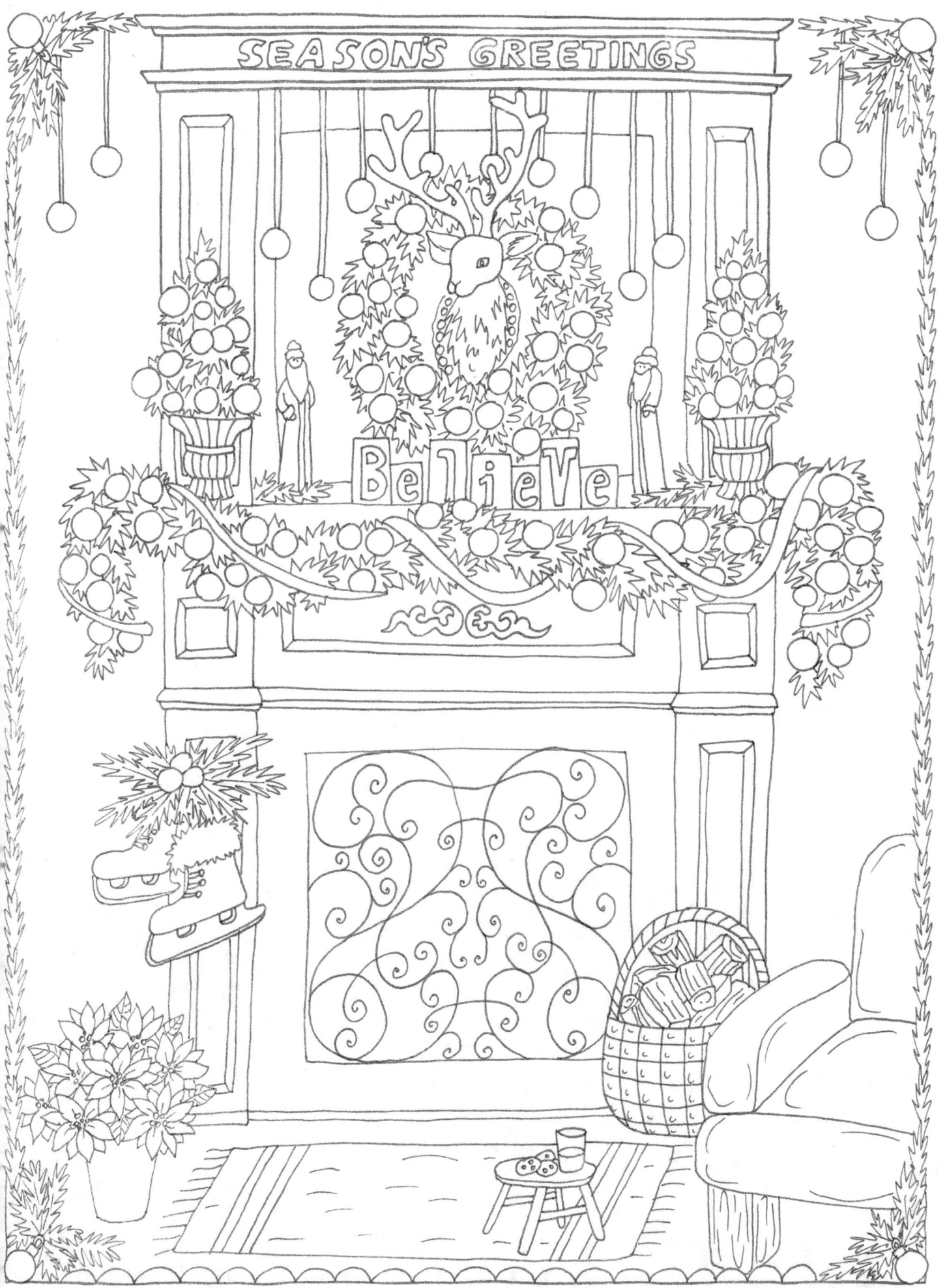

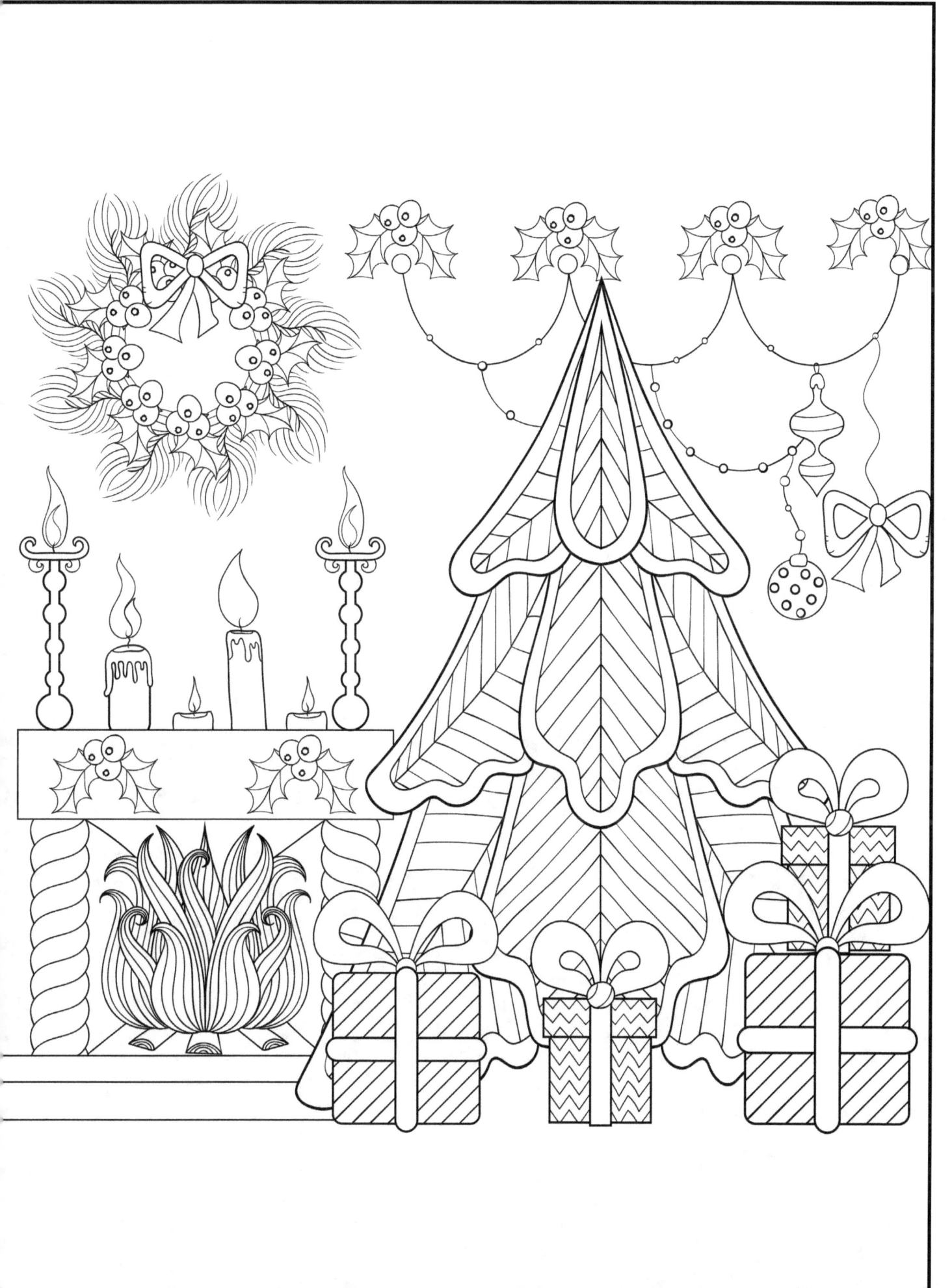

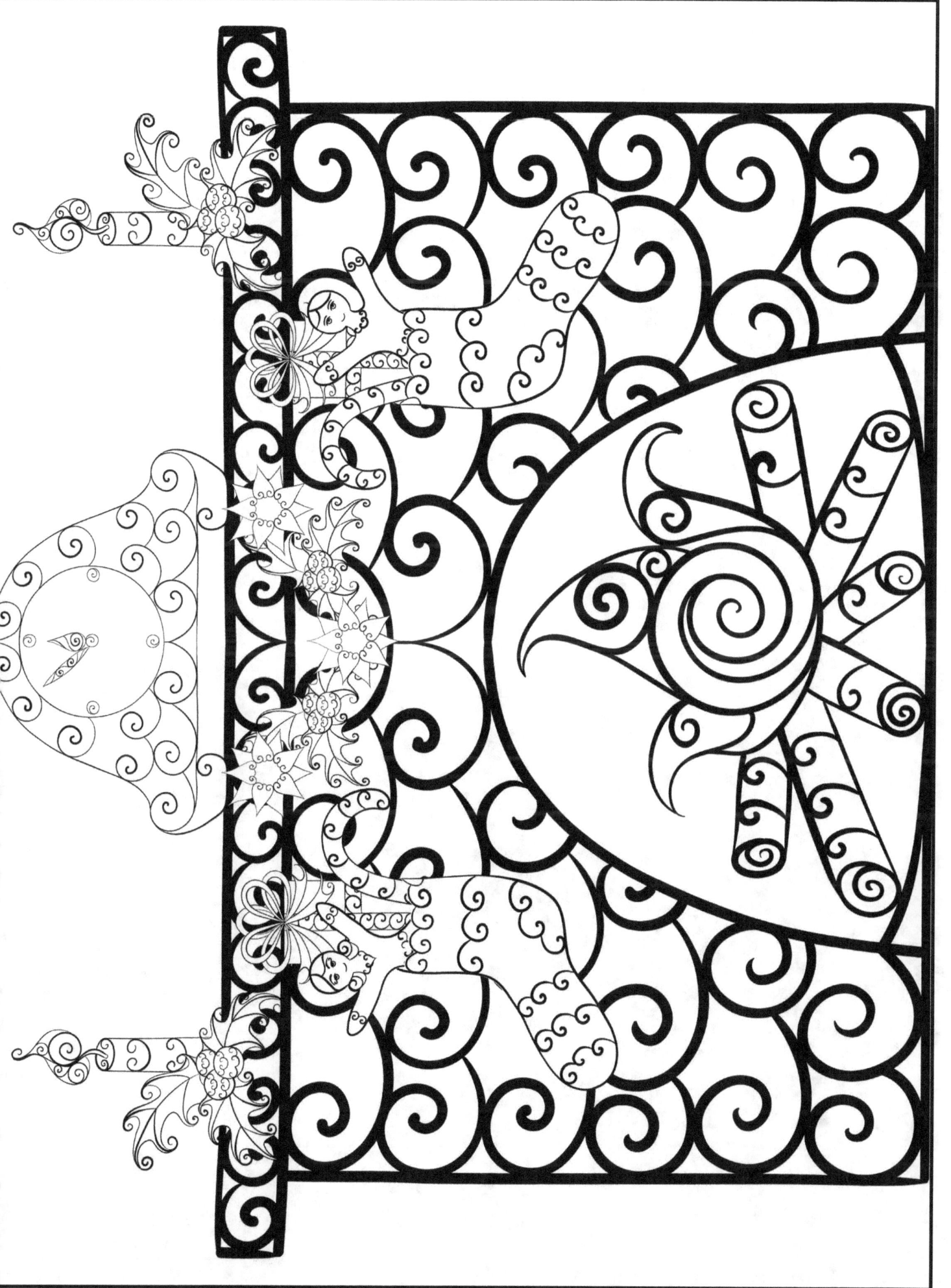

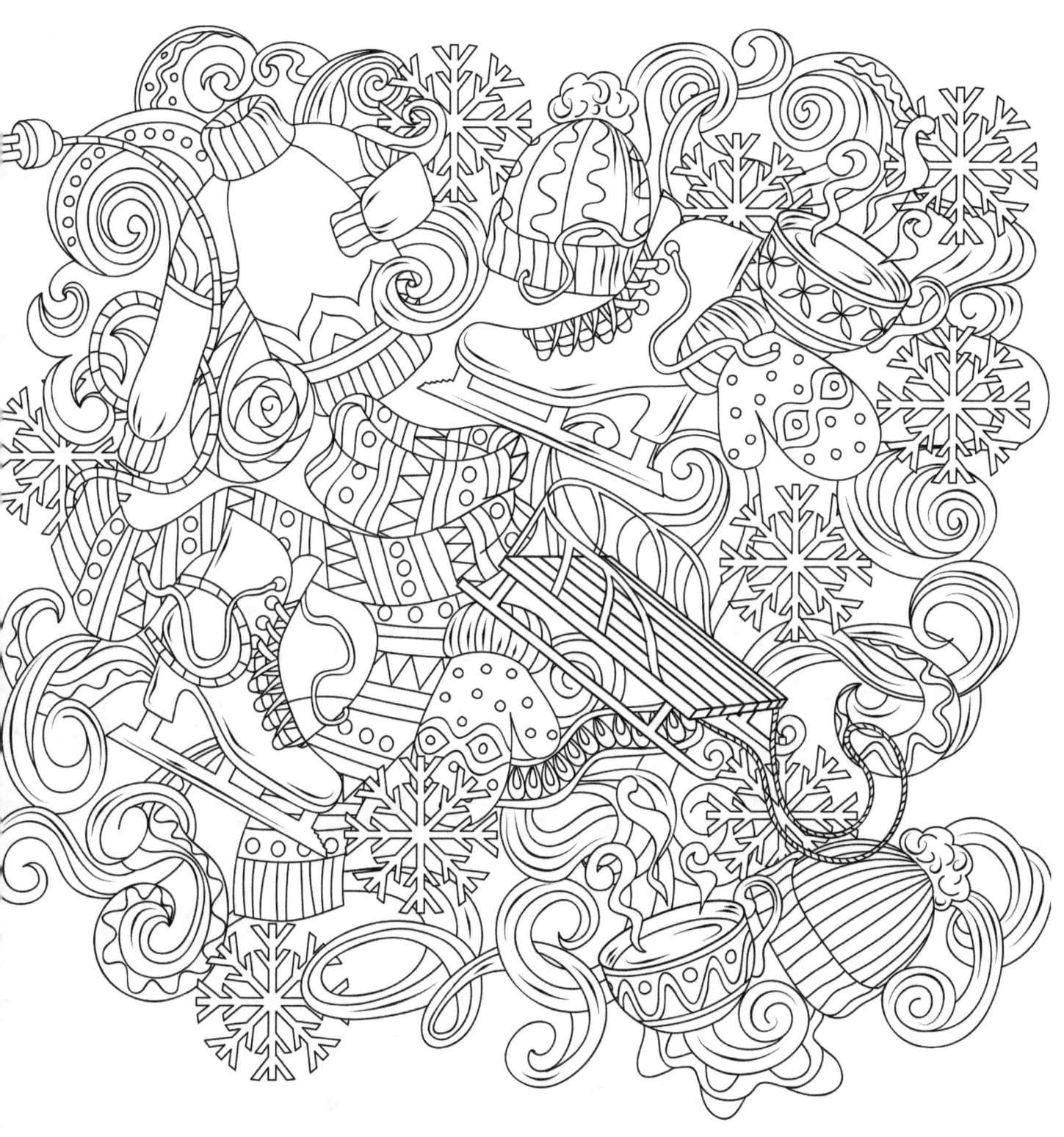

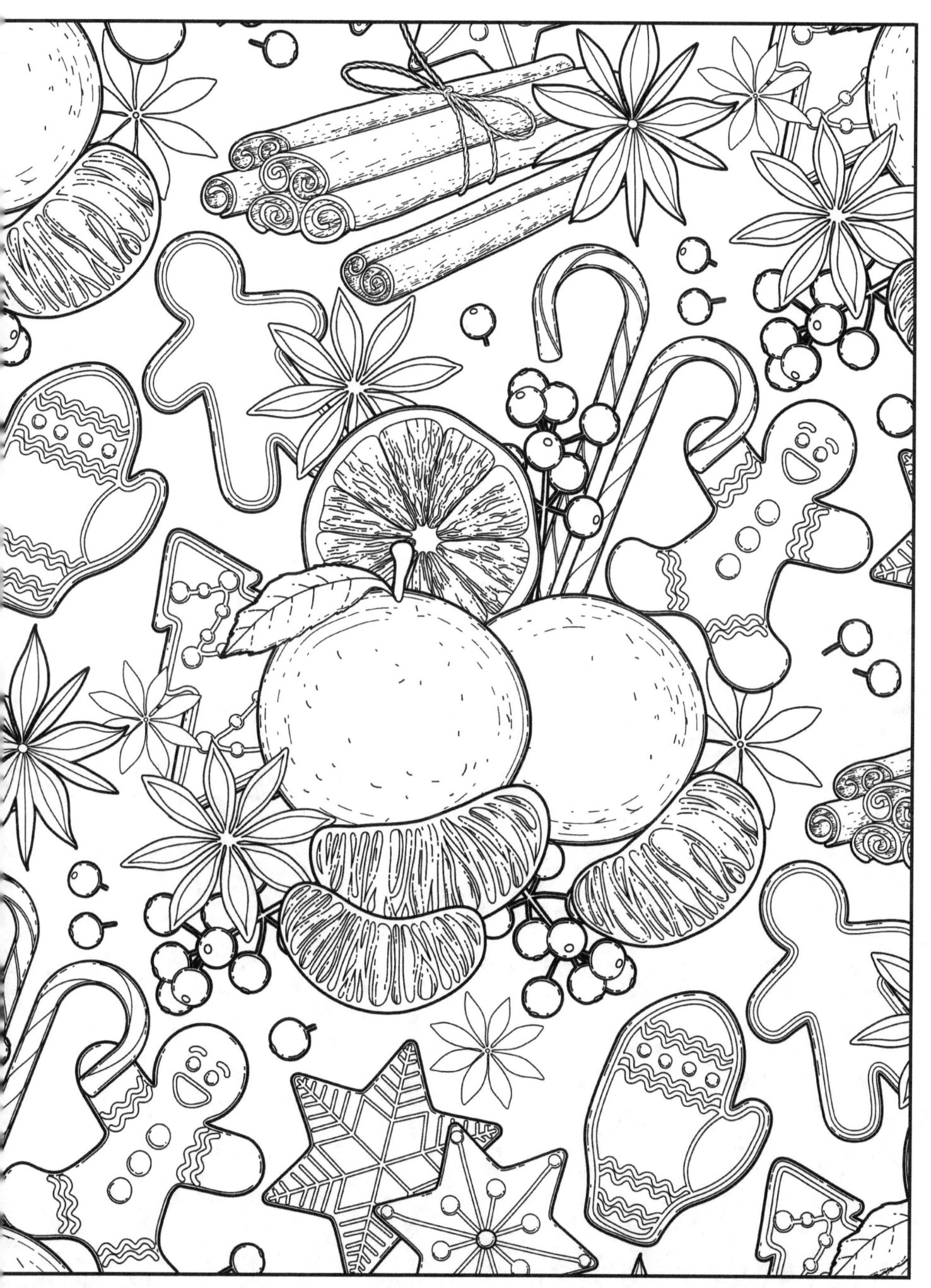

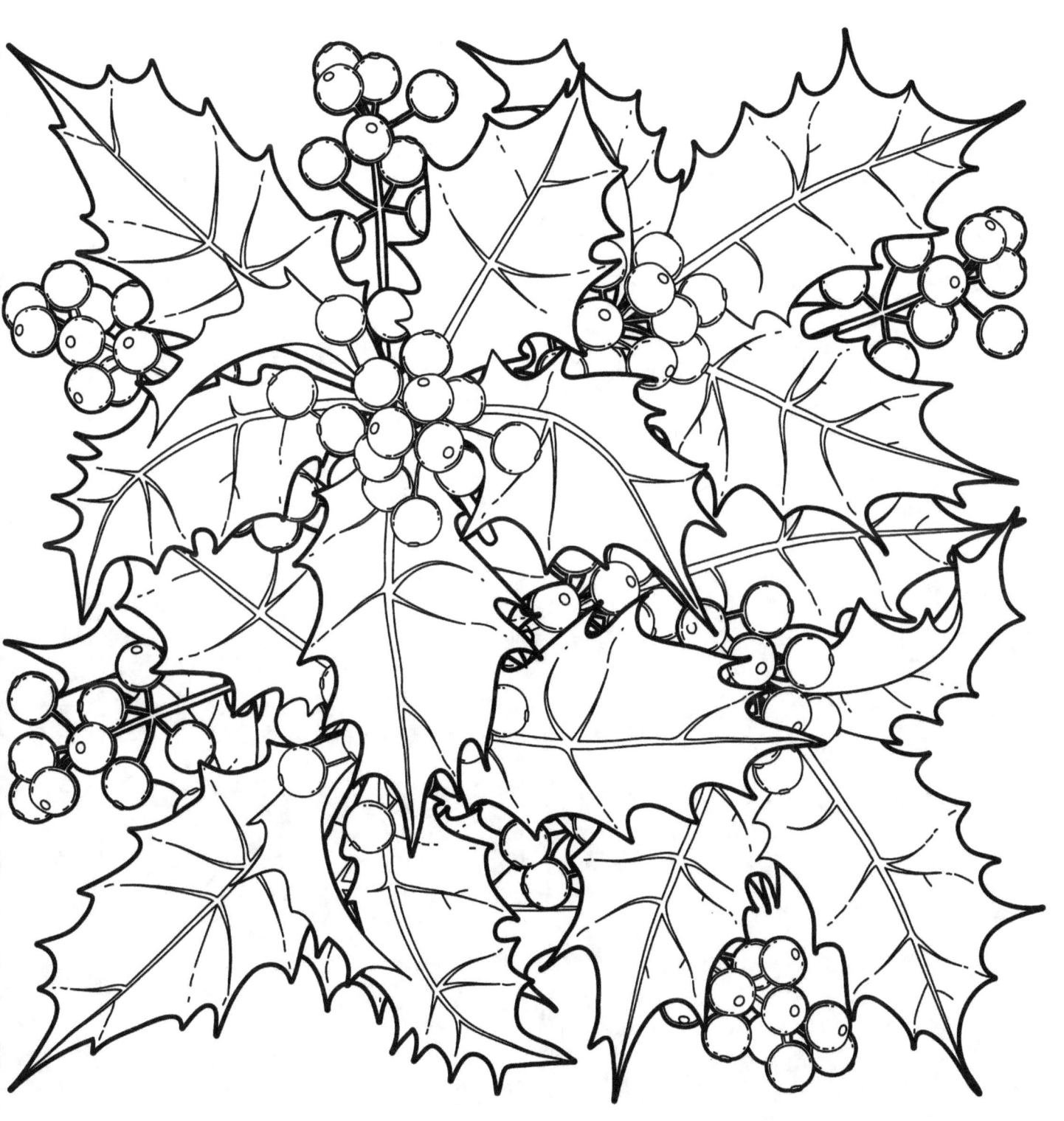

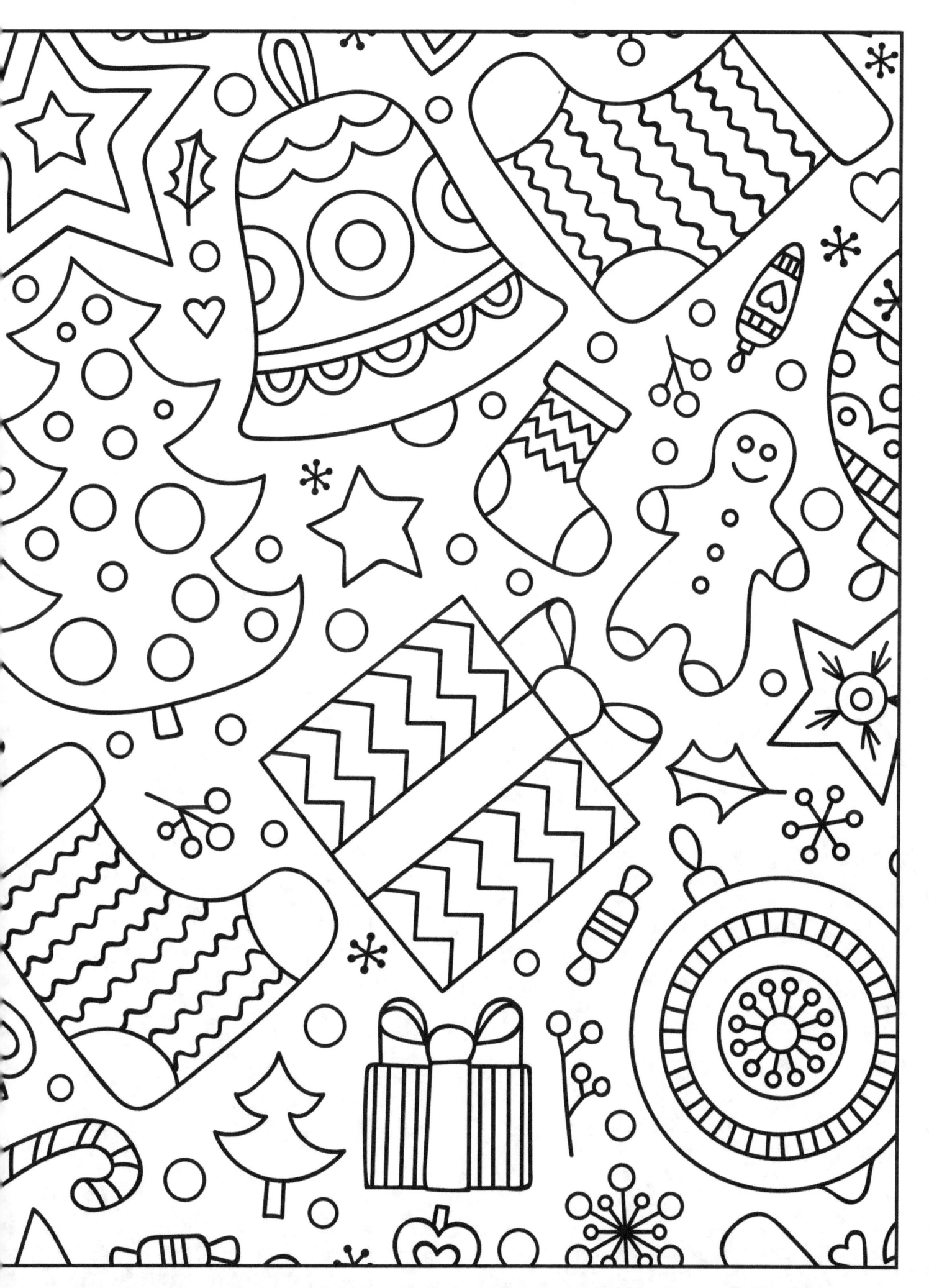

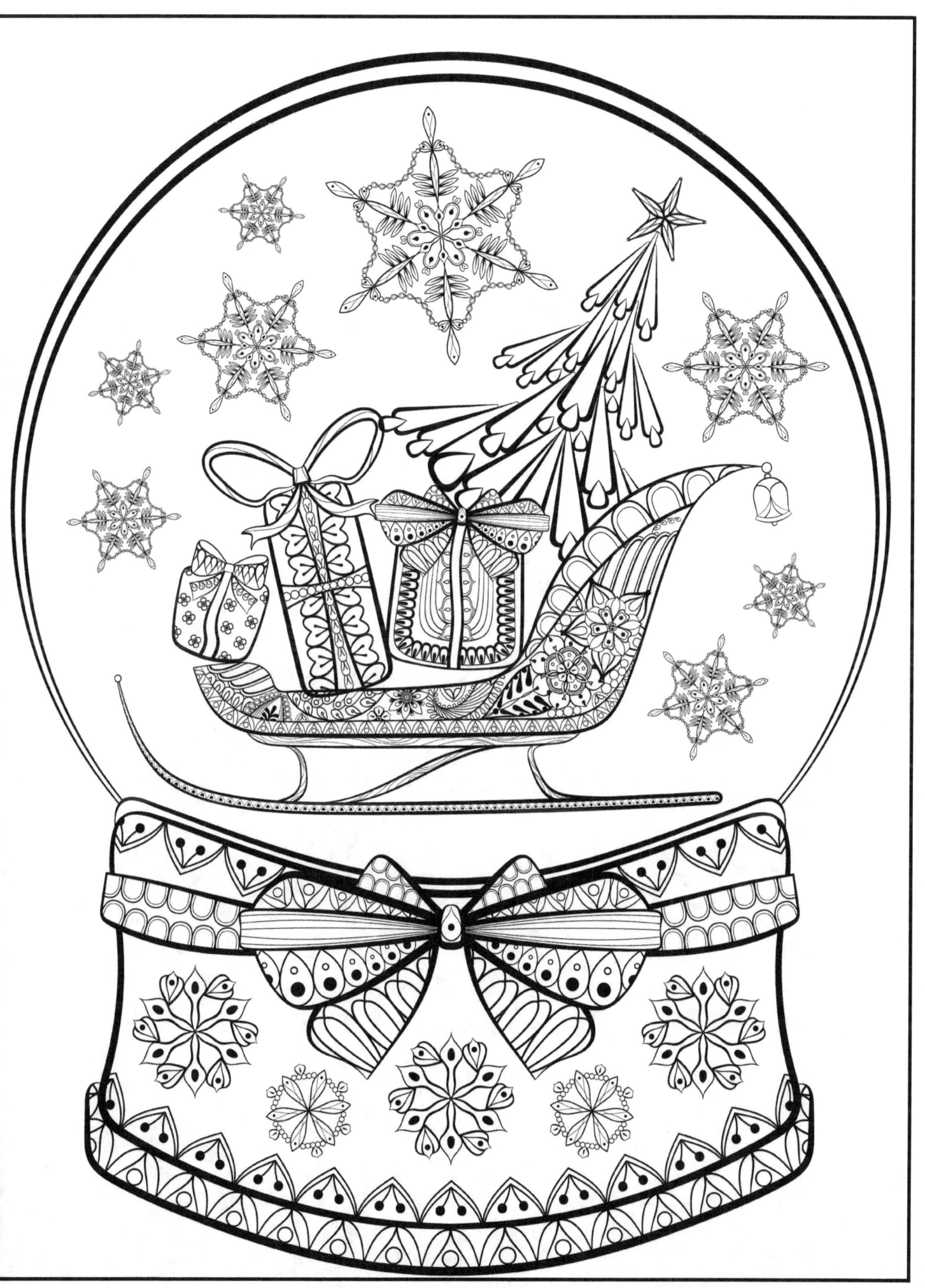

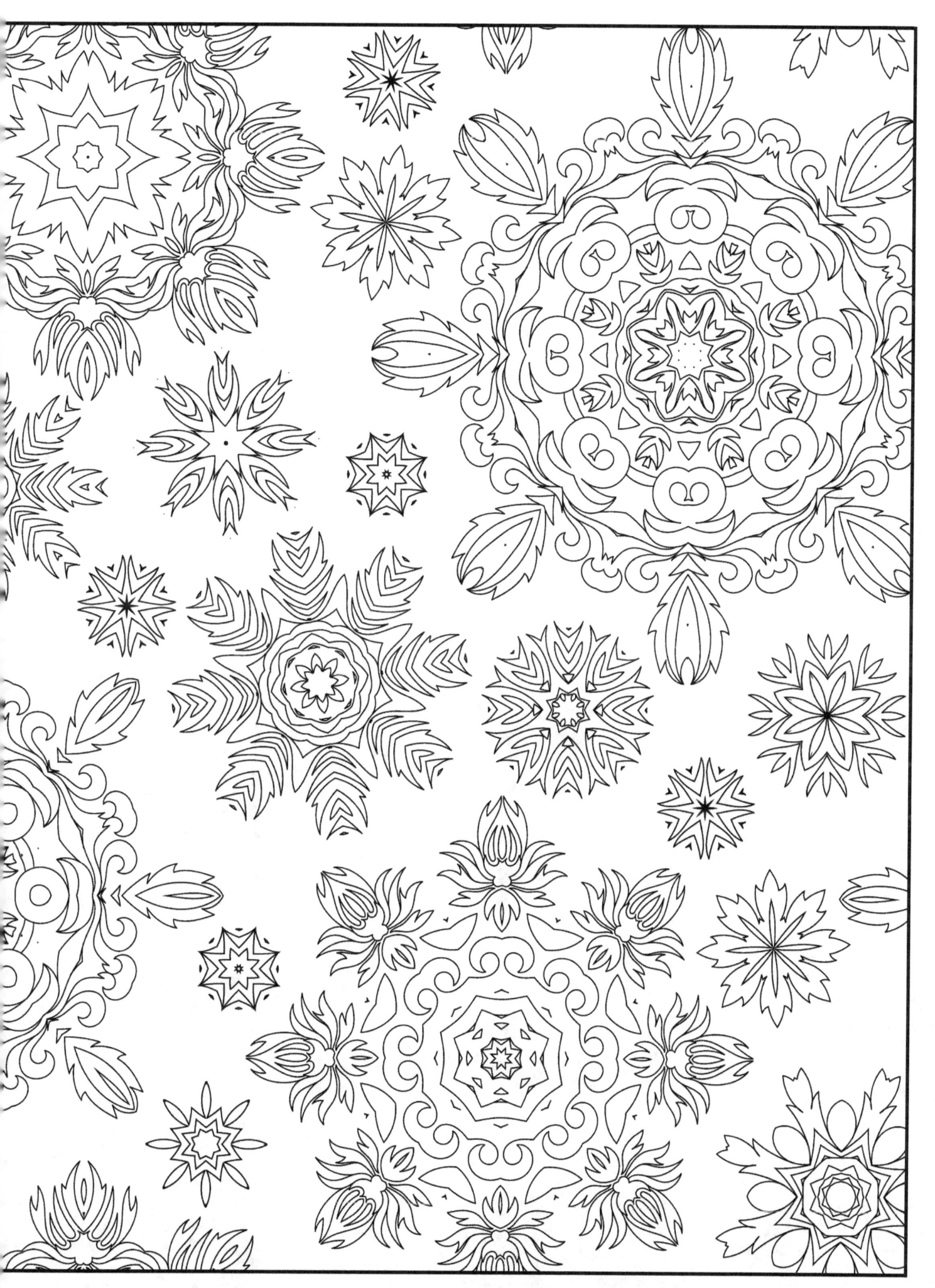

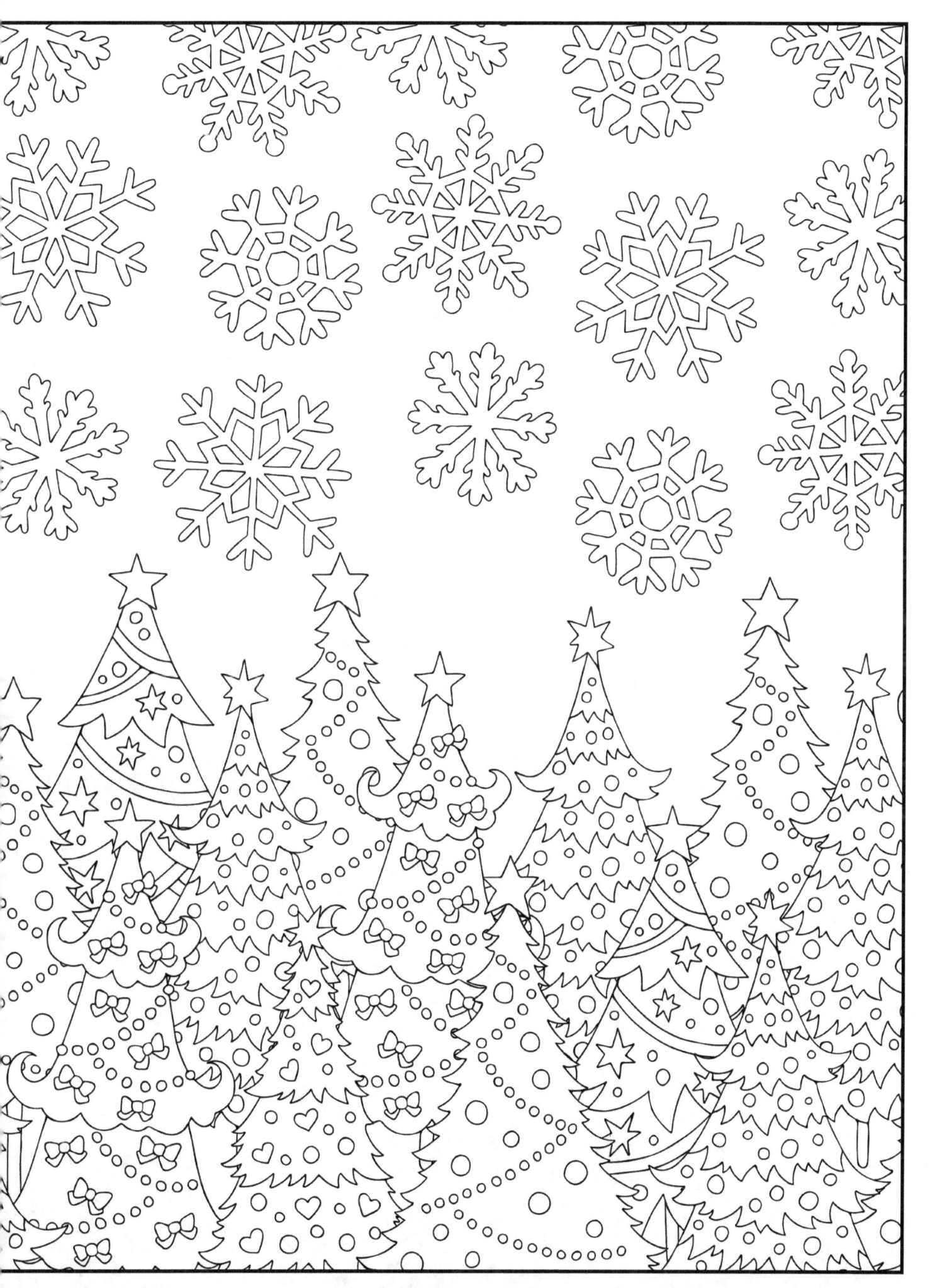

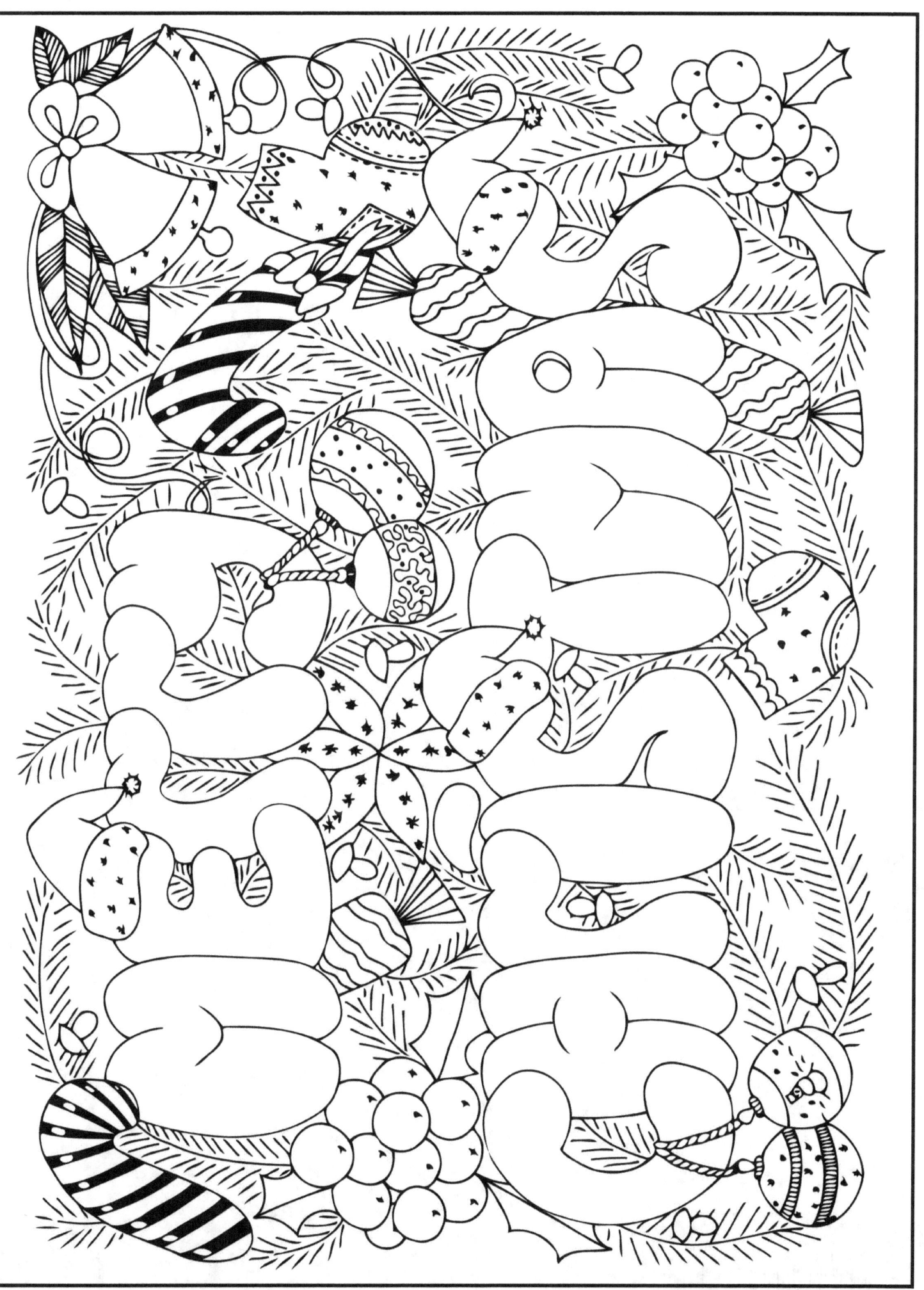

www.ingramcontent.com/pod-product-compliance
Lightning Source LLC
Chambersburg PA
CBHW081609220526

45468CB00010B/2823